SUCCESS

FAILURE

FROM THE BLOCK TO THE BOARDROOM

THE TRACEY D. SYPHAX STORY

AS TOLD TO
DETRIC "QADIRIYYAH" GOSS

Tracey D. Syphax
From The Block To The Boardroom
www.fromtheblock2theboardroom.com

ISBN-13: 978-0-9850295-0-0
ISBN-10: 0985029501
Cover Design by: Detric Goss

Library of Congress Cataloging-in Publication Data has been applied for.
Printed in the United States

SUCCESS ➤

◄ FAILURE

FROM THE BLOCK

TO THE BOARDROOM

THE TRACEY D. SYPHAX STORY

DEDICATION

To my brother Troy Syphax, I write this book in your loving memory. You left us far too soon, and how I wish you'd had the opportunity to see my dreams realized. But I know you had a hand in it, watching over me and directing me along the way. Until we meet again...I love you always.

To my loyal customers, friends, and family, if it had not been for all of you, Capitol City Contracting, The Phax Group LLC, and From the Block to the Boardroom LLC, would be mere figments of my imagination. You allowed my dreams to become reality.

Thanks to my staff on the **"BLOCK"** for showing me I was a power leader in the world of business, which would prove to serve me well as I entered the **"BOARDROOM."**

Thank you to my current staff for tolerating me and standing strong regardless of the shifts in the economy.

For the countless people I cannot name individually for fear of leaving someone out, I say thank you. I thank you for inspiration, encouragement, belief in my ability, subscribing to my network, and allowing me to touch the lives of your children. But most importantly, thank you for allowing me to **GIVE BACK TO MY COMMUNITY!**

To my partners, Darren "Freedom" Green, and Detric "Qadiriyah" Goss, who have worked tirelessly through edits and changes to make this book a reality, I say thank you. To Wendy Dean, I say thank you for your hard work. To my friend and consultant, Glenn Townes, I say thank you for your hard work and dedication to this project. To one of my best friends, Jim Golden, who happens to be the ex-police director of Trenton, New Jersey, I'd like to say thank you for your support and encouragement. To my friend, brother, confidant, business partner, and mentor, John Harmon, you are a jewel to be treasured and I appreciate all you have done for and with me.

To Reverend Simeon Spencer, my Pastor, friend, spiritual advisor, and mentor, I'd like to say thank you for your guidance and for lending an ear over the years. I'd also like to acknowledge my Union Baptist Church congregation for being constant supporters of my life's mission.

To my Mom, Nancy Syphax and my Dad, Frank Syphax who unknowingly encouraged me to be determined and successful.

To my mother-in-law, Ruth Gibson who has been my second mother for more than 30 years, you have provided shelter when life rained down on me with incredible force and you never wavered. You remain a source of strength and shelter for me and I know I can come inside whenever the temperature changes. Thank you for loving and supporting me, flaws and all. But most importantly, thank you for raising such a beautiful woman, who I am honored to call my wife every day.

Thanks to my wonderful children, Trachell Unique and Marquis D'Andre, for making me feel like I am the best father in the world. Trachell, I see your strides and watch you follow in your mother's footsteps and every time I see you, I still see "my little girl." Professionally, and as a parent, your growth is **INSPIRING.** To my boy, Marquis, you are your father's child, and I am proud that you have allowed yourself the opportunity to grow through life's lessons. I see you prospering, striving for a better you and my heart smiles knowing that you are becoming the man YOU always wanted to be. I'm PROUD of you Son. I love you both beyond words.

To my best friend and wife, Margaret Syphax, you are my biggest cheerleader, critic, mother of my two children, grandmother of my two precious granddaughters, Brooklyn and Sanaa and backbone of my very existence. If every man were as fortunate as I to have a partner and soul mate like mine they'd be blessed! I thank God for you daily. Thank you for your patience and for being the glue that has held the Syphax family together for over 25 years. Thank you for knowing me better than I know myself most times. You are what it means to take a man's rib and create a wife especially for him! You are my rib and I would lie down my life for yours. Margaret, I dedicate this book to you and thank you for being the best wife and mother <u>this man</u> could ask for.

Tracey D. Syphax

CONTENTS

Tracey D. Syphax

INTRODUCTION

What does it take to go From the Block to the Boardroom?

I was a knuckle-headed shoe shine boy who sold newspapers. It was the late 60s, early 70s and there really wasn't a lot to do in Trenton, New Jersey. I needed a come up from shining shoes and cleaning windows in downtown Trenton. So I thought about it. My family roots were thick in the illegal business. I come from a long line of hustlers and thugs and it was time for me to close the generational gap and get back to where I came from…**THE BLOCK!**

I needed a plan, a method, a vision and that would require additional thought. I spent long nights masterminding my introduction. I spent many a day studying the streets. Who was moving what? Who was controlling what and how hard was it to out maneuver the police?

Who were the suppliers? Who were the runners? Who was getting it and who was merely getting by? Most importantly, how many of these hustlers could I trust? I mean really trust? After a considerable amount of observation, I disappeared from the shoe shine and window cleaning world and reemerged **"THE MAN OF THE BLOCK**." In the same manner in which you see Clark Kent disappear and reappear as Superman, my transformation was realized. Shoe shine boys chase women, baiting them with what they have in their pockets, which is most likely just enough to buy dinner. I no longer needed to bait, they followed me as if I was the Pied Piper. I was a **HUSTLER**, and I had no intention of going back to shining shoes!

My life was changing and it was going to resemble Heaven in my eyes, just long enough for me to get comfortable and forget about how HOT

HELL actually is. **WELCOME TO THE BLOCK**

Somewhere my life took a turn towards the legal side of success. Maybe it was because I barely survived being shot accidently by one of my partners in crime. Perhaps, it was one drug coma too many that prompted me to change my ways. It could very well have been the many talks with my grandmother who told me that God would find me in my darkest hour. Whatever it was, I was tired. I was tired of hustling, tired of jail, tired of running, tired of drinking and drugging, and just plain tired of life.

I longed for legitimate success, the kind that would make me a household name for something other than having the best dope on the streets of Trenton.

My success did not come easy and I'm not proud of a lot of things that I've done in my life. I've done things that hurt many people, while making bad decisions that could have cost me my life. Nonetheless, it is because of these harsh and brutal realities that I am the man I am today.

It's because of my experiences that I believe you can make it just as I. I share my story with you in hopes that you will understand that even when the **BLOCK** seems like the only way out of a bad situation, the BOARDROOM is always as option.

WELCOME TO THE BOARDROOM.

FROM THE BEGINNING TO "THE BLOCK"

The day I was born JFK was at Rice University in Houston Texas speaking about putting a man on the moon, while somewhere in Asbury Park, New Jersey I was being pushed onto this earth. September 12, 1962 Tracey D. Syphax the son was born. Today, Tracey D. Syphax the man is going to offer you a front row seat in what has molded me into the individual and humble human being I am today. If you ask my wife she'll say I'm a great husband, father and provider. My kids would tell you that I am now a dedicated dad, who at times was too involved in their adult lives, but only **I can tell you who I truly am**, the mistakes I've made, bad judgments, hard times, and roads I've paved, to then be redeemed through God's guidance and LOVE. **So let's start at the beginning.**

I don't come from money. Although, if you research the Syphax family tree, you'll see that our family history dates back to George Washington's wife. Syphax must have been the surname of my father's father, because my grandmother's surname was Tucker. I only had the opportunity to meet my

1

grandfather a few times as a youngster and even still I didn't understand our family's history. It wasn't until I became an adult that I began to understand the lineage and legacy connected with the Syphax name. We knew nothing about any of this when I was coming up.

We were poor and relied on state and family assistance from time to time. Yet, we were kids, and kids will generate some kind of fun regardless of their economic status. When I was younger, I spent a lot of time at my Aunt Barbara's house. She is my mother's sister and when we weren't" living there, her house still remained the place to "hang-out" with my older cousins, Byron and Gregory. We called Byron "Kid Dynamite" and Gregory was affectionately known as "Shoes". However, my closest friend was my brother Troy. He was such a free spirit; much more outgoing and social than me. I was quiet, serious and very subdued. I can only assume that the differences in our personalities played into our strong connection. Troy wasn't my only sibling; he was just my full blood brother. I'm not even sure if people still refer to their siblings as half or whole, but I know that Troy and I were connected in a way that made "**us**" different.

Even though I was born in Asbury Park, Trenton is all I know because my mother moved back to Trenton after her and my father separated. I was only 3 years old and Troy was 4. By 1968 we were all living in Miller Homes, which was located in East

Trenton. When I say "All", I mean me, Troy, and my Aunt's Barbara's kids. I remember looking up at those very tall buildings and thinking, "Wow, that's a lot of windows." People in the neighborhood didn't know which kids belonged to which sister, but they knew we were all related, and they looked out for us all the same.

On the sunny morning of May 29, 1969, kids were out in the courtyard playing as they usually did. Troy had a school trip that day and it would have been like any other except for the fact that Byron was in St. Francis hospital because he had fallen off a roof in the back of the Miller Homes. Troy and several friends were heading to the store to grab a few sodas for their field trip and decided to race to the store. A friend recalls Troy dodging between parked cars in an attempt to get to the store first. The friend suddenly realized that Troy wasn't behind him. He turned around only to see Troy lying in the street. He had been struck by a truck. It was a horrific accident and the streets were soiled with blood, glass, and fluids which marked the streets as a reminder of what had just occurred. That scene…the image of where my brother died was a constant reminder for me and replayed in my dreams for many a nights following the accident.

A neighbor rushed to the laundry room where my Aunt Barbara was washing clothes and told her one of her children had been hit by a truck.

Remember I told you they couldn't tell the sisters apart, they just knew we were all related. My aunt came running towards Lincoln and Seward Avenues and people on the scene were screaming not to let her see Troy like that. Two men held her back kicking and screaming, at times lifting her off the ground to hold her until the ambulance came and transported him to Helen Fuld hospital. My aunt was the first to run through the Emergency Room doors only to be told that Troy was pronounced DOA. My mother arrived shortly after to hear the devastating news. **Her son was dead.**

My brother was gone and I don't remember who told me he had died. I just remember the somber mood of the family and the effect it had on my mother. I believe that day served as the breaking point for her. For years she'd been suppressing many hardships and personal violations. With the death of my brother she slid deeper into a dark depression. My father arrived at the funeral home and had my brother's body transported to Asbury Park. My mother was livid. She felt like Trenton was his home, because that is where she was raising us. A small viewing in Miller Homes was held for those who wanted to show their respect and condolences for my family's loss.

After Troy got hit, several riots incited. People had complained for years about there being no stoplight at the corner where the accident occurred, and this would be the tragedy that would force the City's hand to finally address those complaints. This would be the first time I'd witness a neighborhood join forces for change. I had no idea at 7 years old how that movement would serve me well later in life. People were marching, sitting in the middle of the street, and refusing to let traffic pass, until someone realized the severity of the situation. A boy had died! The City placed a blinking light at the intersection and it didn't take long for the empowered community of Miller Homes to come together and tear that blinking light down! The people wanted; no they demanded a **standard functioning traffic light!** There were so many people participating, yet out of everyone involved, my Uncle Buddy was the first and only one to be arrested. When he appeared in front of the judge, he was told he would be made the example and the judge proceeded to incarcerate him on the charge of inciting a riot.

It took almost two years, but eventually a fully functioning traffic light was placed at that intersection, where it remains today. There have been no fatalities at that light since my brother's death.

It all proved to be too much for my mother. The families weren't communicating, as I'm sure blame was being placed and it just all became too heavy of a burden for her to carry. So once her and my father's divorce was final, she packed us up and at the request of a male friend, moved to Texas. This was going to serve as our time to heal. However, the healing never happened because not long after our Texas arrival did trouble find us again. I didn't know of my mother's dealing with drugs until much later, but it seems that this incident in Texas was in direct relation to that addiction. She was placed under arrest and I was immediately placed into foster care. My foster parents were not very loving people. They had several foster children and I vaguely remember the details of their home, but I do remember where I slept. It was a big empty room with two bunk beds on each side. I had to be about 8 years old, and although my mother and I had counseling to help us cope with our loss, it was obvious that the counseling had not been helpful. Losing Troy made me feel like I'd lost a piece of myself. Now, here I was in this strange place with these strange people, experiencing my first true emotional set back.

Although my stint in Texas was short, it was long enough for me to get molested by my foster sister. I do not remember her name, but I do remember her being around 24 years old and not living in the house. She would return to the home to assist my foster mother with the children and although I was only 8 years old at the time she obviously found me very attractive. It wasn't fondling or just touching, she introduced me to full blown sex! I never told anyone about it until well into my adult life, and still, I only shared the information with my wife and a counselor who was helping me to deal with a few issues. My mother and family will hear of it for the first time through reading these words in this book. I believe I didn't talk about it because I didn't understand it. Thinking back to her, she wasn't a bad looking woman, so I still don't completely understand her actions. I've come to accept that she must have been suffering from a sickness to think that it was okay to violate a child.

It wasn't long after being placed in foster care that my Aunt Barbara was called. I don't remember if it was because I was acting out or what, but she was immediately making plans to come and retrieve me. Not sure of what to do first, she turned to the man she was dating at the time, who just so happened to have a lawyer friend in Texas. The lawyer was able to handle the case for my Aunt and get me back to New Jersey without her having to come to Texas. Now, some will say that the friend being in Texas is a coincidence, but I am more of the belief that it was God. There will be several more coincidences in this book and I'll chalk them up to God as well, because HE can be the only explanation.

I returned from Texas and was back in Miller Homes with my cousins, but this time I was living with my Aunt Barbara. Being back in Miller Homes made me think of Troy often; wondering how my life would have turned out had he not been hit that day. Even today, I still ask myself would I be the man I am if he were alive? Would I be better? Could he have saved me from myself at times? Or, would I have somehow sucked him in as I had others because I was so influential? All questions I'll never know the answers to, but I honestly believe he helped guide me out of some of my darkest moments. I believe that God sent him to watch over me and with every success I achieve, I celebrate it as a victory that belongs to the both of us.

It didn't take long for me to start acting out once I was back on familiar ground. I was harboring secrets that were playing out in my actions. Soon my mother was released and she too returned to Trenton and moved in with my Aunt Barbara. I started stealing and committing other petty crimes to ease my pain and mask my emotions and with each passing year I delved a little deeper into more criminal behavior. The older I got, the more reckless I became. I was cutting class, smoking weed, and being a total nuisance to the Trenton Public School System. My most memorable moment in school involved meeting the girl I knew I'd marry in the 8th grade at Junior 3. Her name was **Margaret**... but that's the beautiful side to this story and you'll hear about that later in her words.

By puberty, life was different. The realization of my mother's drug addiction was apparent, and she was turned out. My mother was my first true introduction to **drugs, the life and substance**, which

8

was followed shortly by my cousins introducing me to **drugs, the game**. I started out light, as most introductions do, and eased my way into it. I was the "weed joint seller", like loosey cigarettes, and then I graduated to nickel bags. Before you knew it, I was on the New Jersey Turnpike headed to New York with my mother, her boyfriend, and my cousin to buy weight. I was only 15 years old. A short time later I enlisted the assistance of my big cousin Shoes and we became fast and furious in the weed game. Although Shoes was older, I was more of an influence on him than he was on me. One of my strongest memories from that time is an incident where I was on the train coming back from New York alone crying like a baby because Shoes had been arrested for selling weed to an undercover cop. We were going to New York to cop some weed. To this day, I do not understand why he brought weed with him knowing we were going to cop. I remember it like it was yesterday. We got off the train and he had about six or seven bags of weed on him. We hit 42nd street to pretend to shop just in case we'd been followed by the police. New York is known for their undercover sting operations and we walked right into one. As we walked down 42nd street, we were approached by a stranger looking for some weed. In true junkie like dialect, the stranger asked, "Ya'll got some reefah?" Shoes being Shoes says, "Yeah, yeah, I got some reefah,"and served the junkie like 3 or 4 bags. Money in hand we continued walking down the block. All I remember is looking at the guy and thinking that he walked like

9

the cool cops on T.V. with the too tight jeans. You know, he had that Starsky and Hutch strut. Before we knew it, we were surrounded by New York City Police screaming at us to "GET DOWN!" They arrested Shoes for selling weed to an undercover officer and sent me packing towards the train station to head back to Trenton alone, but not before taking all of our money because they said it was drug proceeds. I cried through just about all the stops. Looking out the window along the way...Rahway, Metuchen, Metro Park to Princeton, I cried. I knew he was a cop! He walked like a cop! However, that experience didn't deter me, because I was right back in New York not too long after that incident with Shoes coping weed again.

If you're wondering where my guidance came from, let me remind you that my relationship with my father was strained. My mother was more like a colleague in the game with a habit than a mother, so there was no parental guidance.

My first time being incarcerated as a teen landed me in Mercer County Youth Detention Center (The Youth House). The Youth House was a jail for juveniles. The police who worked there knew me personally and gave me special treatment. I'd sit up front with them, watch TV and drink coffee all night. I didn't learn one thing from the experience because the stay wasn't rehabilitating. Hell, I held the keys to my own cell! The guards would say, **"Tracey, go lock yourself in!**

The guidance I did receive came from pimps and hustlers at least 15 years my senior.

My mom started working at Claitt's bar on the corner of Stuyvesant and Exton Avenues. She convinced the owner to give me a job. I was 16 years old with false documents saying I was 18 just so I could bartend. At the time, the legal drinking age in New Jersey was 18. The drug game had assured me that shining shoes and cleaning windows was well behind me. It also allotted me a huge following, and this was something new. My personality and sharp dressing only accentuated what I had to offer. I was packing Claitt's with a full house every weekend. I even got Shoes a few hours of slinging drinks as we ran our drug business out of the there. I was tending bar and learning business skills at the same time. I learned all about bookkeeping, cash flow, and how to complete an Accounting sheet. What I didn't realize at the time was this was truly my first introduction to running a business.

Word traveled fast that me and Shoes sold the best weed, and that I was packing Claitt's Bar. It didn't take long for a pimp name Jay Morgan who had recently purchased Vivian's Pink Chateau, to come calling. He wanted me to come and work for him. He approached me, and I explained the situation

I had at Claitt's to him. He didn't care about that; he wanted me on his team immediately. So I left Claitt's, and started working for Jay. In true pimp form, he was a sharp dresser with big cars and a wonderful way with women, while I was still very young and impressionable. His girl at the time was a beautiful young girl name Pearl, who happened to be Margaret's older sister. She wasn't one of his prostitutes, but he was definitely trying to bait her in. I recall him making me watch one day as he beat her beyond recognition in front of the bar. That left such a bad taste in my mouth and put my perception of "Pimping" in such a bad light. But that's how Jay was; he was arrogant and very inconsiderate of others. I remember watching him sit at the bar and burn $100 bills for no reason other than the fact that he could. I mean he hit the street number so often and for such large amounts of cash, that maybe he felt that he had money to burn. He hit the number one day for $68,000!

I remember when this man from New York City happened upon the bar. After ordering a few drinks, he offered Jay some of his cocaine to test. Jay went in the bathroom, took a hit, and said the man's product was garbage. He then proceeded to flush the man's cocaine down the toilet. He was something else, but above that he was business savvy when it came to running bars and women and I was a quick study.

Jay never really liked Shoes, and once Shoes started dating Pearl, that dislike turned to hate. Jay supposedly disrespected Pearl one day, but I don't recall exactly what it was he said or did. Now I need you to keep in mind that at this time Shoes was only about 19 and for all intent and purposes was scared to death of Jay. I mean his reputation preceded him, and one was wise to be fearful. We were all down at The Annex Lounge across the street from what is now Maxine's, which at the time was a gay bar called Casa Lido's, and one of Jay's associates says, "the two of you have to fight." So they go outside and Shoes puts the pieces on Jay and knocks Jay out. Jay is laying under a car, basically sleeping, Shoes grabs Pearl, I grab Margaret, and all the other bystanders take off running afraid to be around when Jay arose from beneath that car.

By the next day, word on the street was that Jay was looking for Shoes for retaliation. Since I worked for Jay in his bar for a short stint, he definitely should have known who I was when he saw me. However, on this particular day, I was heading to Margaret's house and once I arrived, I knocked and they let me in. Unbeknownst to me, Jay was parked outside the house like he was on a stake-out! He'd been calling Pearl repeatedly to come outside, I knew nothing about that either. I was just coming to see my girl. Well, from wherever he was parked, he assumed that it was Shoes entering the house and not me. Every time he'd call Pearl would stress the fact that it

13

was me and not Shoes, but Jay wasn't buying it. He demanded that Pearl send me outside to prove that it was me. I wasn't worried about it. I figured I'd go outside and he'd see it was me and drive off. I walk outside, and he whips the car up on the curb. The action startled me so bad that all I could do was stand there frozen. In one quick motion he jumps out the car, whipped the gun out his pocket, and placed it firmly to my head. He's screaming at me to get in the car, so I did. Once I'm inside he pulls off quickly, leaving skid marks in the street, and smoke in the air. We make it to our destination, which happens to be Kingsbury Housing Project and he picks up the phone and calls Margaret. He instructs her to have Pearl come outside to talk and for her to bring some cash. I can't even remember the ridiculous amount of money he was requesting. Now if this were an episode of Starsky and Hutch, at that moment the door would have burst open and I would have been saved! But this wasn't television and he wasn't acting. He was behaving so erratically that I didn't know what he was capable of at that moment. Love makes people do crazy things and he was obviously in love with Pearl. Unfortunately for him and me at the moment, the feelings were not mutual.

Margaret agreed to give him the money but called the police instead. About eight hours into the ordeal he released me and was arrested. A court date was set and we all testified. He beat the charges because there wasn't enough evidence to convince the judge that I didn't go with him of my own free will. Not to mention, I was incarcerated at the time of our court date and me appearing in handcuffs and khakis was definitely working against my case.

I was reminded of the strange ordeal when an article surrounding Jay's death was written. He was gunned down by a bullet intended for someone else on Martin Luther King Blvd. It was ironic that as my business life was beginning, one block away his life was ending. In typical Trenton newspaper fashion, his entire life was recapped to include his pimping, hustling, and the kidnapping of Tracey Syphax.

By 18, I was lucky enough to be in receipt of my high school diploma, but I didn't graduate or walk with my class. My diploma was hand delivered to me at Mercer County Youth Detention Center by Detective Black and Detective Charles with strict instruction to never enter Trenton Central High School again. EVER! At the time of graduation I was serving time for weed possession. I couldn't even take Margaret to the prom. I always felt bad about that because Margaret was a good girl and deserved the best. She didn't do drugs and knew nothing about selling them and I did my best to keep my drug usage and selling hidden from her. I always blamed someone else for me getting arrested. I needed her to see me in a positive light at all times and I was able to keep her in the dark about my dealings for a long time.

Once I was released from Juvie, I was back in the game heavy. Shoes and I were on a path of higher learning to include the PCP market. We started selling this brand of PCP called "Reverend Ike" out East Trenton on Oak Street. Reverend Ike was it! Everyone in town wanted it and came to me and Shoes to get it. Our name rang bells so loud in the PCP market that the Spanish dope boys down in South Trenton, who liked to smoke PCP, started checking for us on a regular. Every day they'd pull up in one of their Datsun 240Zs with the T-tops pulled back, sporting their big gold chains, and buy some of our PCP. Again in true Shoes fashion, a relationship developed and we started hanging with the Spanish boys to learn the dope game. Next thing you know we were dope dealers down in South Trenton in the evening and PCP pushers in the morning out East Trenton.

It doesn't take long before cockiness turns to foolishness and a drug dealer will think, "I can try it just once." I did, and before long...he who was the dealer was now the biggest user of his own supply. The cardinal rule of, "Never get high off your own supply," was like many other rules I didn't follow. I was young and impressionable and to some degree a follower. If the Spanish boys were wearing herringbone chains, I went and purchased a herringbone chain. They drove Datsun 240Zs, so my first car was a Datsun 240Z, and like every junkie I'd come to encounter over the three years I'd been in the game, I was now turned out. I was sniffing dope and coke and constantly moving from location to location because paranoia steams heavily from narcotics. So here I was moving massive amounts of drugs from hotel to hotel running from the police, when they probably weren't even on to me yet.

By the time I was 18 I was homeless. However, I was an 18 year old homeless person with a lot of clientele who could buy my supply. I even had a few well-to-do clients in New York City. I would jump on the Turnpike and go up there to party and provide goodies for the elite. Poor little black boy traveling all the way to New York to supply their habits. I recall crashing at this white model's apartment for about five days of partying and drugging. As I stared out of her window on the 120th floor, I remember saying to myself, "How the hell did I get here?" I actually asked myself that question a lot.

There was this one time I was taking a trip to New York to cop drugs in a powder blue Corvette that belonged to my girlfriend's mother. My girlfriend was eight years my senior and she knew my profession. She liked to sniff heroin so she would give me the keys freely to make drug runs to New York. At least once a month I was driving up the Turnpike in a T-top convertible thinking I was made of brand new money.

One night during the cold winter of 1980, I was in New York with Jo-Jo Mamon, who I was dating at the time. A few weeks earlier Jo-Jo had introduced me to this beautiful white model that lived in the city. This particular night she was staying in a swanky hotel. Jo-Jo and I decided to go hang out with her. Although her career was winding down, she had graced the cover of some of the most well-known magazines on the newsstand at that time. She was beautiful and I was smitten. Not to mention, they both like doing all the things I liked to do, so we did a lot of things that evening. I needed to pick up a package before morning, so I left them there. I remember leaving the hotel and making my way to 72nd Street and Central Park West near the Dakota building. I saw all of these people and police, but had no idea what was going on. I knew John Lennon lived there through conversations with the model that night. However, I didn't realize that they were there for him at that particular moment. I was in such a drug fog walking through the streets of New York that for a quick moment I thought they were coming to get me. Maybe Jo-Jo had gotten upset and thought I was a little too taken with the pretty model and turned me in. I quickly realized those thoughts were stemming from the narcotics. The next day I found out from the news that John Lennon had been murdered.

Moments in history always remind you of where you were in your life at that moment in time.

18

At that moment John Lennon was dead and through my drug addiction, I was a dead man walking... I would soon be arrested and sent to Yardville Youth Reception & Correctional Center, to start my first bid as an adult. I did two years and headed home in 1982.

CHAPTER 2
The Streets Prepared Me for Business

"Cash is King- A royal tyrant that shows no mercy"

It was 1982; I was home and doing quite well. I landed a roofing job, which would become my trade of choice. The pay was between $11 and $12 an hour, which was pretty good money at the time. I settled down in my role as man and provider to Margaret and by November 1984, Margaret and I welcomed our first child, our daughter, Trachell Unique. By February 1985, Margaret was pregnant again and due to deliver by year end. I proposed prior to the announcement of our new arrival, but with another baby on the way we immediately moved our wedding from the summer of '86 to the summer of '85. Our son, Marquis was born in December.

Life was good. We were happy and doing well and it didn't take long before I was named Foreman on the job. In my new role I was in charge of operations for Virginia, New York, and Boston with my very own 7 to 8 man crew. We would be on these job sites for months at a time. In our down time we would find the local hot spot in whatever city we were in and party the nights away. I remember when we were in Boston for about a month and a half. I decided to put my pimping skills to the test. I learned the pimp game from Shoes. Even though I hung around hustlers and pimps as a youngster, there was something about the manipulation and control that Shoes exhibited when it came to women. I was always the better hustler, but Shoes was a master manipulator in the pimp game. One night I met this young white girl who instantly fell for me and my style. After a few weeks, I learned she was a prostitute. I took advantage of that new found information and put her on the stroll for me. She would bring me the money right to the hotel room where I was staying. That scene was so heavy, so vibrant, and so filled with liquor and drugs that I quickly, without warning found myself getting high again. Once my habit kicked in, my focus became doing what I had to do to supply my habit. In the past, hustling was the answer and now it was the answer again. However, this time I was going to use a different approach.

I sat down one night and thought about how we ran those highways day in and day out, without being pulled over by the police unless we were speeding. I understood that it was because we were a part of a legitimate business. Racial profiling was heavy in NJ back then and a car with two or more black men on the NJ Turnpike was like a red flag for

New Jersey State Police. I started to think about ways that I could transport the drugs using the very same methodology of a **legitimate business**. That night the idea of Capital City Roofing was born. Shortly after conjuring up this plan, I obtained all the necessary paperwork and acquired the licenses and my first **legitimate** business was up and running, well legitimate at least on paper. I was 23 years old.

I purchased a truck, put the company name on it, and hired a few runners who worked for me on the street as my first crew. On paper I was legal. In reality I was anything but.

I hope that as you read this story you understand that I am in no way glorifying what I did, I'm simply outlining and describing it to you so you can truly have an honest and actual depiction of my journey to the boardroom.

The business was up and running and we were running up and down the Turnpike with coke and dope tightly tucked in tar cans lining the bed of the trucks. I used the same knowledge I got from working in the bar at 16 to become a foreman on my first job fresh out of prison. Now, I was going to pull it all together and run my illegitimate business through my legal business.

A street hustler's mentality is directly related to the mentality of a businessman. A businessman is a certified hustler. Even if you have never obtained any business documentation, opened a bank account, or successfully filled out an accounting sheet, **you already have the skill set to run a business!** To prove my point, let me share a few things with you. A successful business is run on understanding and mastering that business" strategies and tactics. A successful business is built and operated on the management's decision to demand outstanding results. It requires discipline, financial management, understanding accounting (money), the ratios of performance, liquidity, efficiency, equity, and most importantly, employee productivity. A successful business is maintained when those who run the business understand the forces that push profitability as they continue to find ways to lower operating expenses. A successful business exemplifies all of these things, while overseeing accounts receivable with a watchful eye. If your business is about selling; you are always seeking ways to increase sales revenue and there should always be a positive return on your investment.

INVENTORY BECOMES
RECEIVABLES = CASH

And you never want to run out of cash! Nor should you just sit on cash and wait for it to magically multiply. Business is about making your money grow. I ask you, in all of the examples I just provided… does this not define what a street hustler does? If you are in agreement, I seriously need you to reevaluate your role!

I ran Capital City Roofing successfully as a front for about 2 years. Now what happened during the course of those 2 years was life altering on its own and would ultimately become my saving grace.

Margaret, my wife, my love, the woman who'd completed a 2 year bid with me, running up and down the highway to Yardville, who'd just birthed my two beautiful children, who'd taken me back countless times was reaching her limit. She was not going to sit by and watch me self-destruct. She loved me, but loved herself and our children more. With those thoughts fresh in her mind, it became obvious that I was choosing drugs over family life. Margaret made the conscious decision to walk away. It was what we called our spring of 1987 "**break**".

What else is there to do "**on a break**" besides get deep into the one thing that takes your mind off of everything else? For me it was drugs and involved selling and using them. I engulfed myself into getting the money to support my habit. One of my regimens was to spend a few hours a day in a crack house as the supplier-on-demand. I sure wish I'd thought about trademarking the "on- demand" concept.

Cable companies across the world would be paying me royalties right now.

One day, no different than any other I'd spent inside the crack house; I was introduced to this very intriguing young woman. I'd heard her name a few times in the street and knew that she had a reputation for being a "REAL" hustler. I liked that. A true hustler in female form was affectionately known as a "ride-or-die" chick during that era and that is what Sherry was. It didn't take long to incorporate her into my illegal business. The more our relationship evolved the more involved she became. I trusted her almost immediately and before long she was carrying the drugs and the pistol. Once she was completely acclimated she was making solo trips to New York and picking up packages alone. She handled the business and I trusted her until the one time she showed me I couldn't. She stole from me for what probably amounted to no more than a half-ounce. After she did it she was MIA for about two or three days. I was searching for her and paging her constantly, but she never responded. I got word that she was home and made my way to West Trenton. I began banging on the front door of her Hermitage Avenue apartment and even though days had passed I was just as angry as the day I realized she had stolen from me. I think I was so upset because she didn't have to steal from me. We were in business together! When she opened the door she immediately began explaining; rambling on with the, "Tracey let me explain, let me explain" and before I could stop her, shake her, smack her, curse her out or anything, she fainted! She dropped to the floor like a bag of bricks! It scared me so bad I instantly forgot about her stealing and tried to revive her. I ran to the kitchen, got a glass of water and threw it in her face! Looking back on it now, I can laugh, because I realize she was just as intelligent as I thought. She faked me out real good with her deceit to mask her deception.

By 1987, Sherry and I had Academy and Centre Streets on the South side and Southard Street on the North side of Trenton locked down. We had about 13 workers and three significant sections of the city locked. Sherry was still handling most of the business and I was okay with that because we'd moved passed the thieving era into an era of admiration and respect. She was in love with me and it's a lot easier to be loyal when genuine love is involved.

By now Trenton was full of drug dealers, crack was not yet KING, but King Pins ran rampant and held their territories respectfully. I didn't really have any competition. I say that because I was a different kind of hustler. There were many individuals who genuinely disliked me, but I was in a completely different category than most of the drug dealers from Trenton. I was a junkie who sold major amounts of drugs. I was still getting high off my own supply and my biggest fear remained not being able to have my drug of choice when I desired it. That thought alone motivated me to keep my hustle strong and that very same thought outweighed the massive amounts of money 10 to 1.

Sherry and I were as strong as the network we built, and although we had minor missteps along the way, nothing major happened to change the outcome of our relationship. That was until the day she shot me. It wasn't intentional; she was trying to shoot one of our workers who owed me money. I can only assume at the time that Sherry considered herself the enforcer as well. I say that based on how the situation played out when we saw the worker and his girlfriend on Southard Street. Sherry screamed, "There they go right there!" She jumps out the car, runs down on them, and starts berating them. "I know ya'll stole the money!" Without warning, Sherry punches the girlfriend in the face and I jump in between them. As I'm trying to break them up, Gerry jumps on me. Sherry lets the girlfriend go and whips out the pistol. She's aiming the pistol, fires directly at us and accidentally shoots me! I just remember hearing the shot, and I have to tell you it's nothing like they make it look in the movies. Getting shot is traumatic, life changing, and it hurts like hell!

I have blood gushing down my shirt and everyone including me is panicking. Gerry and his girlfriend are trying to calm Sherry down because she's screaming hysterically. It's funny how the crisis changed the entire dynamic of what originally happened. Would we have acted in the same manner if Sherry had actually shot Gerry? I doubt it. We most likely would have been running down Southard Street trying to get rid of the weapon. The same weapon which by now Sherry had dropped in the street to run to my side. She was so hysterical that one would have thought she'd accidentally shot herself. I completely understand where her head was at in that moment. In her eyes I was dying in the street and she was the one who'd killed me.

They put me in the car and rushed me to Mercer hospital. At the same time, Dexten who lived on the Blvd swooped in like a bird and picked up the gun. I'm not sure if this was an attempt to assist in hiding the fact that Sherry had shot me, or if he just wanted the pistol. I mean we were all getting high back then, so a gun definitely could have garnered a few dollars.

The entire ride to the hospital Sherry's screaming how sorry she is and telling me not to die. When we arrive at the Emergency Room, the questions immediately start. How did it happen? Who shot me? Who saw what happened? Instantly, Sherry was calmer. She was trying to explain what happened without incriminating herself, but you know someone was going to tell what happened. There are always a thousand people who saw what happened, but their stories differ slightly. However, as the detectives arrived on the scene and began questioning witnesses, they learned that Dexten had retrieved the gun. I guess all the witnesses got that part correct because the detectives took the information they obtained and it landed them directly in front of Dexten's door. Now loyalty is limited, not to mention the history between me, the police, and the block that included Dexten's house. Sherry and I had been arrested at a crack house on the corner of Trent and the Blvd, which was only three doors down from Dexten's house. Someone had called the police and said we had a gun in the house. Sherry had whipped the gun out on someone and when they ran out the house, we assumed that they must have called the police. When the police arrived and began banging on the front door. Sherry and I made a break for the small crawl space in the attic to hide. The Police came right to the attic and instructed me to come down or they were sending the dogs up! I came down; they bust me in the back of the head, and courted me off to jail. But this time was a little different.

The police arrived at Dexten's door and told him that that they knew he was in possession of the weapon and that he needed to turn it over or he would be charged with obstructing justice. Of course he caved. Not only did he hand over the gun, but he confirmed that it was Sherry who shot me.

Back at the hospital, Sherry was not aware that the police knew it was her. I was told that she was panicking because she knew someone was going to tell it. Once the police received confirmation that it was Sherry who shot me, they arrested her and took her into custody. I needed to go into surgery, but because Margaret was still legally my wife, they needed to wait on her arrival to explain my injuries and have her authorize the surgery. They stabilized me until she arrived from Newark. Once there, she signed the papers and they rushed me into surgery. I slipped into a coma and I remained in a coma for three weeks. When I awoke one of the first things I realized was that it was the end of the month. People really do awake from comas and ask what day it is. Of course I survived the shooting, how else would I be sharing my life's story with you? The bigger question is did I learn anything from it?

CHAPTER 3
When GOD came calling...
I answered the Devil

"God is going to find you in your darkest hour and only then will you realize who you truly are"~Elsie Saunders, my praying grandmother

When I came home from the hospital Sherry was still locked up. I bailed her out about a week after my release. Once she was out of jail, we resumed our relationship and the business, which included two to three trips a week to New York City to cop. As soon as we'd sell out, we'd be back on the highway to re-up. We never kept the drugs on our person for long as a precaution to getting stopped and searched. If we were taking long trips, we'd always stop and securely wrap the drugs to be buried over night with markers for easy retrieval in the morning. Yes we were assuming we were smarter than the police, but I can attest to the fact that we **WERE NOT.**

As time passed, I began to accumulate charges. The incident that did me and Sherry in happened several months after the shooting. We were headed back from New York and got pulled over by the police in Elizabeth, New Jersey. They found drugs and a gun in the car. I always wonder if the reason for the arrest was because I was high at the time. This would truly be the end of our life together because I went to jail and so did she. Once they fingerprinted Sherry they immediately brought up the shooting charge on her and gave me the option to press charges against her... I wouldn't. She wanted me to say that the drugs and gun that the officers found in the car were mine to help lighten the blow and possibly take time away from her sentencing...I did. However, it didn't help her too much as she had a few pending charges from previous arrests. Neither of us was released from jail after that incident. We were held until sentenced and began our bids almost simultaneously. We communicated for a while through letters sent between the two penal institutions, but once she got word that I was trying to work things out with Margaret, she stopped writing. I followed suit, which worked perfectly because Margaret had already given me the ultimatum to end the relationship.

It was 1988, I was 26, crack was KING, and I was headed back to Yardville. After 3 weeks in Yardville, they shipped me to Southern State Prison; a newly built facility in Delmont New Jersey. Southern State seemed more like a college campus or country club than a medium security prison. It was beautiful, which is hardly a word that anyone should use to describe a prison. I quickly landed a $1 a day job building storage sheds that the prison sold for profit. In typical fashion, I developed a great relationship with the instructor and before long I was running the wood shed department. In 1989 my younger cousin Billy (Dollar Bill) started his bid for shooting someone five times. He was sentenced to a 15 with a 5 and was 9 ½ months into his sentence. I wrote him to tell him how beautiful Southern State was and suggested that he put in for a transfer. At my next visit with Margaret I told her about the letter to Billy and she immediately replied, "**DO NOT LET THAT BOY COME DOWN HERE AND RUIN THINGS FOR YOU!**" It's not like she didn't love Billy, but we all knew about his temper and bad attitude. However, that was my little cousin, and I wanted to look after him. He didn't know how to jail and by now I felt like I definitely knew how, so I needed him close to look after him.

I will never forget the day Billy arrived. I was in the yard when the transport bus pulled up. When that happens everyone pauses to see who the new recruits, are so to speak. I watched them pile off the bus and then I saw him....Dollar Bill!

Once he was inside we had to coax him out into the yard. There was a look of disbelief on his face that clearly showed he believed someone had made a mistake!

We're jailing and within a few months Billy moved from Unit 6 to Unit 2 where I resided. I was a Power Pro on the $1 a day job now which meant I could hire and fire the workers. I wanted to bring Billy on board, but because he was my little cousin my supervisor was reluctant. He didn't want to deal with the favoritism commentary that was sure to follow. He allowed Billy to sweep up the work area, which would only require him to work for 15 minutes a day. This pissed off the other inmates on the tier, not to mention a few officers who didn't appreciate the way the situation had worked out. One officer in particular, Officer Melton, didn't like the working arrangement or Billy for that matter. They were constantly having words with each other and finally Officer Melton instructed Billy to stay out of his way.

A few days after Officer Melton's instructions were given, Billy was on the phone and Officer Melton walked in and told him to get off. He stated that if there was a problem with that request then Billy should refer to the telephone usage section in his prisoner's handbook. Billy immediately flips into Dollar Bill mode, hangs up the phone and walks over to another phone. He tells the officer, "The rules state I can only be on the phone for 15 minutes, but it doesn't state that I can't start a brand new 15 minute conversation on another phone. So I'll be switching back and forth all day!" More words were exchanged and Dollar calmly stated, "I am not like the other guys around here, I will hurt you!" In any language

34

that's a threat and the officer took it as one! He starts to walk over to the "red" phone. The red phone was like the panic button. You didn't even have to speak into it, simply picking it up would alert the other officers and they would all make their way to the area the call originated. Just as Officer Melton is approaching the red phone, I walk in. I see the Wing Rep is desperately trying to speak on Billy's behalf about whatever has just transpired. I hear him stating that Billy is new and just doesn't understand how things work around here yet. I approach to find out what happened. Officer Melton informs me he is about to put Billy on lockdown for threatening him. Billy, who is still very much in Dollar Bill mode looks at me, turns to Officer Melton and says, "I told you I wasn't like these other guys!" He then looks at me again and immediately without warning attacks the officer. He breaks his nose and knocks Officer Melton out. I'm yelling telling Billy to stop hitting him before he kills him. I jump on his back and everything in an attempt to calm him down, and it's not working. There's blood everywhere and as we take account of the severity of the situation, another inmate picks up the infamous "red" phone and yells into the receiver, "**OFFICER DOWN!!!!**" Billy and I walk to the front, look out the window and see the other officers (police) running across the yard. I turn to him and tell him not to run. I told him to just surrender, but he was so crazed at the moment I think he must have still thought he was out on the street. As the officers were running through the front, Dollar was running

35

out the back. He pulls the bloody sweatshirt over his head and hides. Most of the officers run right past him, but there's always one older, slower officer bringing up the rear. Dollar steps out in front of him, pulls the sweatshirt down and tells the officer, "I'm the one you're looking for." The officer grabs him, but doesn't handcuff him and starts to walk him towards lock- up. The other officers realize that he has been captured and radio the officer who has Billy in custody to hold him and stay right there. They all come running over and begin attacking him. One officer wraps his hand around Billy's neck and starts squeezing. Billy turns to the Sergeant and says, "I can't breathe," and the Sergeant replies, "I don't give a damn if you die!" Billy pretends to go limp, the officer releases his grip and Billy breaks free. Now they all realize he hasn't been handcuffed. He's now in the middle of the compound fighting five to six officers, and they're winning. I come running out with a bunch of other inmates yelling that he's my cousin. I can only assume that they took that as a threat, because almost immediately I was bashed in the back of the head, slammed to the ground, handcuffed, and hoisted in the air by my hands and feet like a human Boeing 747 on my way to lock-up for landing.

They immediately shipped Billy to Bayside State Prison and placed him in lock-up. From there he went to Trenton State Prison, which is the toughest prison in the state of New Jersey. He eventually landed in Rahway State Prison. I on the other hand, went straight to Rahway. **Do not get out of jail. Do not collect $200.** Unlike Southern State which was new, Rahway was 93 years old and nothing like a country club.

They hit us both with street charges which carried serious implications. However, when Billy went to court he told the sentencing panel that I had nothing to do with the altercation and that I was just trying to calm him down and stop him from making an already dire situation worse. They removed the street charge from my record, but it garnered Billy another 7 years to his lengthy sentence. I was still charged and would spend the next 365 days in Adseg in Rahway.

I don't think Billy ever felt bad about what happened to me, but I do believe he felt responsible. I know he was relieved when they removed the street charge and to this day he believes that the year in Adseg changed my life. I'd have to agree with that thought.

"God is going to find you in your darkest hour and only then will you realize who you truly are"

That's what my grandmother told me, after I survived being shot and her hearing of me being back in the streets. That's what she told me as she looked in the face of a grown man, but only saw the little boy she'd expected to accomplish much greater things. Sitting in that cell, I could clearly picture her sitting across from me sharing her wisdom. I was in my darkest hour. After everything I'd experienced, this was it and I was reaching out for understanding.

I picked up the Bible and started to read. During those 365 days I read the Bible from cover to cover. I reflected on my entire life. How I'd been shot and survived, locked-up, locked-down, in a raid, and survived the withdrawals from a dope habit cold turkey.

Matthew 25:36 was the scripture that touched me most deeply. It reads, "I needed clothes and you clothed me, I was sick and you looked after me, I was in prison and you came to visit me." Sitting on the bed in that cell I was spiritually naked before my Father, hungry for the truth and the word. After all that I had been through in my life, God was coming to me in that cell to tend to me directly.

As I watched cars go up and down that Turnpike day after day, night after night from my cell window, I remembered the countless times I traveled that same road and how it led me to where I currently stood, behind bars. I asked myself was it all worth it? At my lowest, I recognized it was not. My wife and children were very different elements of my life than they had been before and it was all based on decisions I'd made; some were very bad decisions. Confined to that 6ft x 8ft x 10ft cell, with one hour of freedom a day is enough to kill a man mentally. Yes, I said freedom because anytime outside of that room, which is the size of the bathroom inside of your home, was considered freedom to me.

"What you know about 23 & 1 locked down underground all day never seeing the sun..." That one line from the Beanie Sigel's 1999 album release **"What Your Life Like,"** was my life. **That was Adseg.** Those 16 words were poignant to me standing there in that cell, gazing out of that window, locked down for 23 & 1 all day never seeing the sun... that was my life. I was in my darkest hour and without warning or knowing, God found me. My grandmother was correct in her prediction. It was as dark as it had ever been and out of that darkness, I was spiritually re-born and the revelation of hope was realized.

CHAPTER 4

My Million Dollar Dream
Capitol City Contracting Inc and The
Phax Group LLC

"Now is the accepted time, not tomorrow, not some more convenient season. It is today that our best work can be done and not some future day or future year. It is today that we fit ourselves for the greater usefulness of tomorrow. Today is the seed time, now are the hours of work, and tomorrow comes the harvest and the playtime."
~ W.E.B. Du Bois

With the year in Adseg behind me, I was shipped to Riverfront State Prison in Camden, New Jersey to complete my bid. Outside beyond the bars the war on drugs was waging and the government was losing. Crack cocaine and heroin still reigned supreme; however, my interests were beginning to take shape in other areas. I became involved with a group, who taught and practiced the ways of African American studies. However, the teachings were more from a discipline standpoint. I assumed it was because we were incarcerated and discipline was required and necessary for survival. The more I learned, the more I wanted to learn. Those 365 days in

Adseg allowed me the opportunity to not only reflect, but to grow mentally, evolve as a man, and recognize my weaknesses. I decided once I walked through the doors of Riverfront that I would seek out something different for my life. I wanted to rise up and stand on my feet, because my decisions in life had crippled and buckled me at my knees for far too long. I would now begin to understand the power of standing strong without looking over my shoulder. Everything that I'd learned was going to pull me out of the trenches and begin to shape me into the man I am today.

I learned of powerful black leaders who were built from that entrepreneurial spirit. Strong black men and women like Madam C.J. Walker, who started in the cotton fields of the South and became an entrepreneur, founding her own business selling Madam Walker's Wonderful Hair Grower. She came from humble beginnings and by the time of her death had established an empire that allowed her not only to prosper and live well, but to give back to the community and lift others out of the trenches.

I was even more inspired by the words of W.E.B. Du Bois, who was the first black to receive a doctorate of philosophy from Harvard University. He was dedicated to the higher education of his race. There was Marcus Garvey who had more of a connection to the African necklace I wore around my neck almost daily than I ever imagined. The pendant which hung from that necklace was the shape of the

African continent which displayed the colors of the African flag. The same flag whose colors symbolized the skin, blood, and the earth as it pertained to the growth of black people.

I studied leaders from the past to the present and happened upon the life of A.G. Gaston. I was taken with the life of A. G. Gaston, a prominent business man, who was named "Entrepreneur of the Century" by Black Enterprise Magazine. I was in awe of his ability to come from nothing, yet before dying at the age of 103, had built, established, and successfully ran more than 5 businesses. He opened his last business at the tender age of 94. I wanted to know how to do that. I needed to understand the blueprint and I was going to use what I learned to establish my very own empire.

I engulfed myself in studying and continued to seek information about successful black business men I had never heard of, which made me reflect upon the ones I did know about. I was beginning to remember what the face of a successful and legitimate black businessman looked like. There were several from Trenton that I remembered vividly. There was Fred "Big Ed" Vereen and Marcus Hill. I remembered many blacked owned businesses like the Turf Club, Big Ed's Supermarket, Supreme Cleaners, Supreme Deli and 4Gs Supermarket. I remembered and then **I realized that the same success was possible for me.** I was beginning to see and understand the concept and magnitude of being a successful black business man who gave back to his community.

I graduated from the program and upon my release from Riverfront was transported to the Clinton House, a half-way house in Trenton. They call it a "half-way" house because you're half way home, but you're still a prisoner. The Clinton House is located at 21 N. Clinton Avenue, only a few blocks away from Miller Homes. I was given a second chance to take the correct path from the very neighborhood I'd taken the wrong path from so many years before.

I had 9 months left on parole and the Clinton House provided the freedom I needed to re-position myself within the community. Prisoners were allowed to check themselves out every day to seek employment, go to the library, or go to the West Ward Center and play basketball. Once I realized I could check myself out, I hit the ground running trying to find employment. I didn't visit any of my old stomping grounds to stay clear of the life I promised was behind me. Not long after arriving at the Clinton House, I lucked up and landed a job with a roofing company. The pay was great, although I didn't see much of it. The Clinton House charged rent based on your income and because I was making good money, they were taking most of it. I held on to that job for the remainder of my time at the half-way house and my employer, who believed in me and my ability, kept me on once released.

I still had dreams of starting my own business and the hours of the roofing company allowed me to slowly begin to put the pieces in place to fulfill my dreams. Each day the other workers and I would start at the crack of dawn, sometimes leaving our homes at 3 or 4AM to make it to the worksite. It didn't matter where the worksite was, we were there. We'd work through lunch in order to have the job completed by 12:30 or 1 o'clock in the afternoon each day. This allowed me the time I needed to focus on building my personal business. I slowly started to build a clientele by completing roofing jobs around the city with the remaining 7-8 hours before the sun set. The first asset of my new business was a small Toyota pickup truck. Customers were referring me to family and friends and the side jobs were coming in quickly. Before long I was working 7 days a week, 16-18 hour days with little time for family. I was killing myself, but I had a vision, and that vision was built upon a strong desire to be my own boss. I knew what I needed to do and the sacrifices that needed to be made, but it was beginning to take a toll on me. In that moment, I needed to be inspired and reminded of why I couldn't quit.

The Million Man March

October 16, 1995

A Segment of the Million Man March Poem

BY MAYA ANGELOU

The night has been long, The pit has been deep,
The night has been dark, And the walls have been
steep.
The hells we have lived through and live through
still,
Have sharpened our senses and toughened our will.

The night has been long.

This morning I look through your anguish

Right down to your soul.

I know that with each other we can make ourselves
whole.
I look through the posture and past your disguise,
And see your love for family in your big brown
eyes...
The ancestors remind us, despite the history of pain

We are a going-on people who will rise again.

A couple of years of being a free man had definitely changed things for me. Early on I'd stumbled once or twice, but Margaret was quick to remind me of what was at stake. Nothing was more important than family and being a provider for my family, so I became more driven than I'd ever been. One day while sitting in the barbershop the discussion turned to **the "The Million Man March,"** also known as **"The Day of Atonement."** It was set to take place in Washington, D.C. with a million black men marching for the sole purpose of being heard. The purpose behind the March was based on the belief that black issues had been thrown by the wayside and they needed to be returned to the forefront so the politicians who were running our nation could address them accordingly. I was more excited about the fact that the keynote address would be delivered by Minister Louis Farrakhan. Despite what others may have thought of Farrakhan, I have always had a sincere respect and a high level of admiration for him and what he stood for. He has always been a source of motivation for me in the sense of self preservation. He stressed it and I believed in it.

By 1995, I had been home from jail for two years. I was working and life was decent, but I still felt as if something was missing. Hearing about a million black men embarking on a journey to Washington, D.C. from all parts of the United States so their voices would be heard was definitely something that peaked my interest. Was this the something I needed? Could this be my inspiration? I began to wonder if it could possibly fill the void of what was missing or at the very least lead me to it. For that reason alone, I needed to be one of those million black men.

I asked my son to accompany me and suggested that he invite a few of his friends along for the experience. My hope was that we would take the trip together and not only learn something valuable from the experience, but would also bond as father and son while participating in something monumental. I believed this experience would be one he could tell his children and my grandchildren. In the future when the conversation turned to that extraordinary day, he could turn to his children and say, "I was there with my dad and we were a part of that movement!"

October 16, 1995 finally arrives and the boys and I make our way to Bus #54. It's a beautiful sunny morning and the air is crisp. As we board the bus, I recognize a few faces from Trenton, but there are many faces I don't know. A level of excitement and positivity is already in the air. Multiple conversations were going on; people were discussing politics, education, economics, the bus was alive with life as me and the boys made our way to find a few empty seats. I don't think the positive dialogue ever stopped as we made our way down 95 to Washington D.C. There was so much to discuss and learn, as I listened to the views of other individuals who looked like me, but thought differently. Men were sharing food they'd packed for the long bus ride and it was just a genuine sense of brotherhood. The entire experience was stirring something in my spirit and we hadn't even reached the mall yet.

Once we reached the mall, the tone of the men changed. It was as if a quiet storm had fallen upon the entire bus. As we exited, I immediately noticed the signs **(Brothers Gonna Work it Out! and It's Our Time!)**, floating through a sea of a million black men. This would be the second time that I would witness the power of unity and what can be accomplished when we come together as a people. I kept thinking about how we were all together, yet there was no fighting, arguing, thug behavior, or animosity. It was one of the most beautiful experiences I'd ever witnessed. I can say it was a definite transitional moment in my life. As I stood there in that sea of men, I reflected upon everything that I'd been through in my life. There I stood, drug-free, gainfully employed, with my son and his friends participating in something positive.

We stood on that mall for more than four hours listening to the many speakers, which included Mayor Marion Berry, who welcomed us to the city, Reverend Al Sharpton, Dr. Cornel West, and Minister

Farrakhan, who closed the event out. The image of different faiths, ages, beliefs, and locations all congealed in my memory in the form of positivity. I will never forget that image.

As we made our way back to the bus the mood of every man onboard was more subdued, quiet. I think everyone was now reflecting upon their lives and how they could take the moment and emotion they experienced that day back home and share it. We all wanted to build upon the mission of our people, carry it back to our communities, and change lives.

WE WANTED TO GO HOME AND SAVE LIVES...STARTING WITH OUR OWN.

I don't think my son and his friends realized the magnitude of that day. Nevertheless, they were present, and I was hoping something positive was stirred in them as it was in me. I didn't say much to anyone on the ride back home. I stared out the window the entire ride, grateful and thankful for how far I'd come. As we got closer to home, night fell upon us and the stars seemed a little brighter. Tears ran down faces in silence and the inspiration I believe many of us were seeking had been received. We were forever changed.

http://www.finalcall.com/artman/uploads/1/mmm1995_003.jpeg

FROM THE VISION OF A MILLION MEN MARCHING

Once back to work, it was back to business as usual with 16-to-17 hour days and 7 day work weeks. Concerned for my well-being and a little frustrated at me not realizing I was killing myself, Margaret gave me an ultimatum; keep the roofing job with the paycheck or step out on faith and start my own business. I needed to sleep on it. In the morning the choice was clear. As a Christian I have come to know that FEAR and FAITH cannot exist in the same place, at the same time. In knowing that truth, I stepped out

50

on FAITH and started my business. Margaret invested $500 and Capitol City Contracting was born.

We started immediately. First, we moved all of the furniture out of the dining room of our affordable housing condominium and turned that area into the company's office. Margaret had purchased the condominium while I was still incarcerated and its location remains very poignant to my story. This is because outside of the front door of the condominium I once laid wounded in the street from a gunshot. This is also the same place I sold drugs for my illegal business and now I was pumping life into this location through my legitimate business. I was officially leaving the block with no intention of looking back.

We ventured out to purchase office equipment and came home with a fax machine and copier. Margaret went to complete the necessary paperwork to incorporate the business. Incorporating the business was an important element in the process because this would serve well for credibility and liability purposes. **In business you always want to protect yourself and your investments from lawsuits.** My corporation is a separate entity and I am an employee of the corporation. After incorporating, we obtained the appropriate licenses and insurance. All that was left was establishing a crew. I had previous experience in setting up a business from my Capital City Roofing days, so I was very familiar with a lot of the processes and procedures. However, this time I was actually the owner and operator of a legitimate business.

My first hire was my brother-in-law, Todd "Blue" Singletary. Blue was a hard worker who always gave 110%. I couldn't understand why he had been laid off from my old roofing employer. Initially I was a little disturbed at him being laid off, as black men were sparse at my old company. However, their decision to let him go was beneficial to building my business. In addition to hiring Blue, I hired a guy with a very strong residential roofing background. He actually had more experience than me in the residential arena and his expertise would be beyond valuable. I came from the commercial side of the business. The final step was to connect with the SBA (Small Business Administration), which is a government funded organization that offers free programs explaining corporate structure, payroll, taxes, benefits, and all the fundamental information necessary to create and run a successful business. Their one-on-one counseling sessions walked me through the entire process from start to finish.

Our first year in business resulted in a great return with the company earning around $22,000 in net income. **Net income** is the amount of revenue remaining after all of your expenses have been paid. Each year we did more and more, and by the third year we netted $180,000. Our 4th year, we earned $380,000 and by the 6th year we reached $600,000.

The business exploded in 1999 when I garnered a connection with the Mercer County Black Business Association (MCBBA). For a young man who thought at an early age that he wouldn't amount to anything more than a common street hustler, junkie, and convict, this was astounding. To turn my life around from drugs to this was truly commendable, and yet I remained humble.

As my business was growing, Trenton was privileged to have its first black mayor in office. Former Mayor, Doug Palmer, spoke very highly of me and my business successes over the years. This was not due to the fact that he was in my pocket or because I was contributing large sums of money to his campaign. He spoke highly of me because I was a young black entrepreneur in the City of Trenton who was establishing myself as a successful businessman, and honestly there weren't a lot of us at the time. I thought it necessary to address that fact because any work that has ever been completed by my company for a project that involved the City of Trenton was built entirely off the honest business ethics of the organization I built. We did and continue to do great work, and that speaks for itself.

As I'm continuing to build Capitol City Contracting I'm constantly thinking of ways to expand the business. Using the same methodology of the entrepreneurs I read about while locked down in Riverfront, like Madame C.J. Walker who expanded her hair care products business to include barber shops and nail salons. I recognized that many businesses are by-products of well established businesses. The closest thing to the construction business in my eyes was real-estate, and I liked the returns one could net in the world of real estate.

As it pertains to business, there is nothing more beneficial to the life of that business than its assets and leveraging those assets. How well you leverage will dictate that organization's growth. I knew if I started buying real estate I could leverage that property and become engaged in bigger and better business opportunities.

I heard about an 11-car garage for sale the owner was basically giving away at $36,000. I researched the property and examined whether it would be a beneficial investment for my company at the time. I believed it was as I needed somewhere to store all the company's physical assets (equipment, trucks, etc.), as well as obtain an actual office location for the business. Margaret was more than ready for us to move out of the dining room space of our home. I purchased the property and immediately started paying down the mortgage. The equity in the building placed me in such an excellent position to embark on other business dealings. **LEVERAGE**! By

2001 I was ready to establish my second business entity and in that year The Phax Group LLC was established. I liked the real estate business because obtaining and selling merchandise was something I'd done for years. Plus, I was never of the mindset to rent property from anyone. I've always looked upon renting as throwing money away. I was more inclined to own and make my money work for me. That's smart business; while you're asleep your money should still be working. The 11-car garage that I purchased for $36,000 is now worth $75,000 with the remaining mortgage balance somewhere around $12,000. I could easily sell the property that has more than doubled in value in 10 years, pay off the $12,000 balance, and walk away with a $27,000 profit. **That's business!**

After acquiring the garage, I quickly realized it was not conducive to our office needs. I would need to keep looking for space so my wife would be able to have family over for dinner in our dining room from time to time.

Directly across the street from the Night Life bar in North Trenton where I used to sell drugs out of, down the block from Dexten's house where police recovered the gun from my shooting, and down the street and around the corner from where the police had once pulled me from a crawl space in the attic, was a little hair salon on a corner lot. This hair salon was owned by an older woman who was a staple in the North Trenton community. She lived and operated her business out of that location for as long as I could remember. One day she called and made me an offer I couldn't refuse. She was retiring and before putting the property on the market, she offered it to me. Over the years she'd watched me change my life and build my business. Now she wanted to offer me a location to house my office. Coincidence...maybe, but all I knew for certain was that I could acquire the building, rent out the upstairs of the property, and allow that income to pay the mortgage. Finally, I'd have an office location that didn't involve me sharing the same space as my personal kitchen. I was SOLD! Business was great! Home life was wonderful, but I was back to feeling like something was missing. It was time to extend my reach beyond my current customer base and begin to give back to my community. As any great entrepreneur will tell you the greatest feeling in acquiring wealth is being able to share it. Giving back is how we grow. My community taught me everything I knew. It provided me the street smarts that helped me survive both in and out of prison and now it was opening its arms to welcome me so I could put my business sense to use.

I needed to show my appreciation not just to my community, but to Trenton as a whole. I didn't know where to begin, but I wanted to make sure that it would have a profound impact. I turned to the strongest connection I've made since entering the world of business. I encountered him for the first time when I became affiliated with the Mercer County Black Business Association (MCBBA) and he has become one of my strongest mentors and advocates in the fight for rebuilding the City of Trenton. I needed guidance, so I called on Mr. John Harmon.

CHAPTER 5

Politics, the Boardroom, and John Harmon

My introduction to John Harmon wasn't one that involved an immediate connection. I'd seen him at functions as I began to affiliate myself with more professional people. Still, I didn't know him. I later learned that John had watched me from a distance since 1998, paying close attention to the choices I was making in reference to my business. We didn't start to interact with one another until I became a member of the Mercer County Black Business Association (MCBBA). I was also extremely interested in getting involved with the Metropolitan Trenton African American Chamber of Commerce (MTAACC) whose mission is "to empower African American businesses through *advocacy*, *education*, and *networking*." I believed that this affiliation would assist in the development of my entrepreneurial goals. However, it would seriously affect my involvement in the MCBBA, because it seemed that both organizations were working on the same black issues for black businesses, but from different perspectives. I had a tough decision to make as I was heavily vested in the MCBBA. However, the organization was much more political than I assumed, and I was nowhere near prepared to enter the political realm without first tackling and understanding all aspects of business.

I was establishing myself as a professional, yet I wanted to stay true to who I was as an individual. In being so committed to my plan and future development, I took on a membership with the MTAACC and retained my membership with the MCBBA. This was challenging to say the least, but the new membership allowed me to get to know John from a professional perspective, and see just how genuinely committed he was to helping others reach the next plateau of their professional careers. Initially from a personal perspective, all I knew about John was that he was a dedicated member of the community who fought for black businesses. From a professional standpoint, I recognized that he exhibited the characteristics that I wished to possess, and that he understood, better than many, the importance of giving back to the community. I was eager to learn how to capitalize on that kind of knowledge. I wanted to know how to become more successful and remain charitable to those who assisted me in that success.

CASH FLOW CONTROLS
THE DEAL

With my membership in the Chamber (MTAACC), I was introduced to the fundamental tools of a successful business. This is not to say that my business wasn't successful, but it wasn't in- line with what was required to take it to the next level. This was also an opportunity for me to work with a black man who was interested in the profitable development of another black man.

One of the first things that John shared with me was the truth in how cash flow controls the deal. The dynamics of cash flow are simple, it basically consist of the operating, investing, and financing activities of a business. **Operating** is the day-to- day operations of the business, **investing** is the buying or selling of assets or investments to build the business, and **financing** is where the money is acquired to manage and maintain the business. Within each of these activities lie one of the most important factors to building a business, and that's networking.

Networking is necessary to build a successful business relationship on local, regional, national, and international levels. Three of the most important associations developed in networking are the relationships one must obtain with a bank, an excellent attorney, and an incomparable accountant.

The bank relationship is necessary when deals arise that need to be financed. **The attorney bond is key** to assuring that your business dealings are unquestionable, and lastly the accountant should be credible in his or her ability to oversee where the money goes and how it's accounted for.

As I applied the lessons from John and the Chamber, he then introduced me to the **Subcontracting concept.** When I started my business I wanted to hire the entire neighborhood. I believed that in doing so, I was giving back to the community. I was very interested in facilitating a continuous charitable contribution to the City of Trenton. At the time I didn't understand how hiring an abundance of people could have a negative effect on the business as a whole and significantly impact the profit margin. The Subcontracting concept allows for an increase in the company's profit margin, at the same time decreasing the company's liability. I was now equipped to use the networking skills I'd obtained to assist other businesses on projects I was managing. This concept is a win-win for all parties because instead of dominating the market, I was now allowing other businesses to grow under my leadership and freeing up my personal time to become more engaged in other activities. This is when I started to pay more attention to what was developing politically in the city.

To do business in any city, a business owner needs to know who the key elected officials are within that city. As John pointed out, it is not so much about becoming an elected official as it is important to have an understanding of and access to the elected official. At this point, I was engaged and ready to tackle bigger professional deals. However, most of my strongest opposition and resistance came from individuals who looked just like me.

By the time I'd reached this level of understanding in how a successful business flows, it was quite easy to look back to 1998-1999 when I established my membership with the Chamber and recognize the worth of that membership. I paid an initial $1250 for my membership. This included the annual $250 membership fee and a $1000 founding board member fee, which served as an investment that was shared by 20 other founding board members. This opened the door and provided the necessary tools resulting in my business being well north of $2 million dollars in assets. I was beyond ready for the next **BIG** thing.

There were several small deals congealed under The Phax Group umbrella and I was very proud of those developmental projects. However, when I approached John about a $7 million dollar opportunity to develop 21 foreclosed properties around the City of Trenton, I myself was a little skeptical about whether I could pull it off. Again,

John reminded me that the deal is **ALL ABOUT THE CASH FLOW**. It doesn't matter how big the opportunity, as long as one can meet their monthly obligations. We worked the deal while John ran an analysis on my ability to acquire a $7 million dollar real estate deal for a quarter of its worth. Based on that analysis, I offered the bank .20 cents on the dollar for the properties with very little out of pocket cost. How could I make such an offer? It again relates back to **cash flow.**

Now here's where it gets political, because we had the money to close on the deal, we needed to work with the city because the properties were foreclosed. The owner of several of the properties had acquired quite a few liens. To my surprise some of these liens were placed on the properties by the owner himself. This would result in him receiving some form of money from the sale even though it was his properties being foreclosed upon. This was a quick lesson on how the game is played. The deal was becoming more and more difficult to close. It would require me coming out of pocket to cover the mounting legal fees to clear the liens and I didn't want to go that route. The other alternative was to seek government assistance.

We decided to look into the government assistance program, as most cities have significant amounts of money and resources available to attain abandoned properties. We made some phone calls to the current Mayor and he seemed eager to get those 21 abandoned properties back on the tax rolls. This gave hope to the project and meant that the deal still had wings. We pulled together a proposal on the 21 properties and submitted it to the City of Trenton. However, instead of assistance, we ran into opposition once again. The Mayor truly was not interested in the deal and although the Economic Development Department offered $100,000 towards the deal, it was short of the amount requested. We were somewhat baffled by the small amount as we'd seen them provide upwards of $900,000 to white developers for a single property that would benefit only one neighborhood. These 21 properties were spread throughout the City of Trenton and would have a greater impact on the city as a whole. The possibility of $5,000 in tax revenue for each property meant an additional $105,000 per year for the city. However, **we got nothing**… so we walked away from the deal.

Was this clearly an example of a black elected official or administrative government having the opportunity to assist a black business owner and for whatever reason choosing not to? I'll let you be the judge of that.

We went back to the drawing board to assess what our next move should be. The commitment from the bank was still there. The money was still approved for the deal, although the deal had fallen apart due to insufficient funds to cover the existing liens. With that information in hand, we repositioned ourselves and John went back to the bank. He proposed a deal for $1 million dollars to be used to obtain a different set of properties with the same profit capacity for The Phax Group. Ultimately this deal proved to be better than the initial $7 million dollar deal. We were now set to begin closing on some of the properties. This deal had no government assistance and went through with little opposition.

As recent as last week, with today being the eve of the 10 year anniversary of 9/11, we received an email from the same bank that's currently financing the $1 million dollar deal. This is the same bank that was set to finance the $7 million dollar deal. The email asked if The Phax Group would be interested in a $15 million dollar deal where I would serve as General Partner and also provide property management services for two buildings in the City of Trenton. How did this deal come about? The same way the $7 million deal came about from those $100,000 business deals I'd acquired before meeting John. One must remember that once you successfully close on one major deal, other deals will begin to find you.

THE TRUST FACTOR

I am a firm believer that one has to practice what they share as an absolute truth with others who are seeking out success; otherwise their words are merely words and hold no weight. John's words have always been consistent and his actions are always in direct alignment with his words. That's very important to me.

Early in the establishment of our business relationship an incident occurred that solidified our relationship for me. It brought about credibility to John's character and I've never questioned it since. John had asked me to attend a meeting with him and another gentleman to discuss a few issues with the Head of the County Economic Development for Mercer County. This being one of my first business meetings with a high ranking public official, I hurried out and purchased a brand new blue business suit and some hard bottom shoes. I of course wanted to look the part. I was eager to understand the inter mingling of the businessman and politics. We were invited to the Head of the County Economic Development for Mercer County's office and were immediately joined by another county official. I don't recall the purpose of his presence or his name, but there was a clear understanding that he was to play a part in the conversation. The purpose of the meeting was to discuss the level of contracts that were being allocated to the African American business owners in Mercer County. The conversation began cordially with everyone introducing themselves and speaking in turn to be respectful of the present speaker having the floor. I was silent and taking notes. As the conversation progressed, one of the county officials said something disrespectful and before I knew it, John had jumped to his feet, slammed his hand down on the table, and told the guy he would come across that table! Here is this 6 foot 4 inch, 250 pound black man stating without hesitation, "Don't let the suit fool you, I'm from **North Trenton** and I will whoop your ass right here in this office!" I was stunned for a minute. I'm sure the expression on my face spoke volumes as I watched it play out in front of me. The room fell silent. I sat up straight in my chair and waited to see what would transpire next. The entire time I'm thinking to myself, "That's my **MAN** right there!" I was impressed! In that moment John clarified what he would and would not allow to take place during the meeting; the tone of the meeting was reset. The meeting was adjourned shortly after the outburst. However, there was a clear understanding that respect was to be shown and provided no matter the dress code.

John's love for the City of Trenton is evident because he's from Trenton. Being born, raised, humbled and developed on these streets of North Trenton, he was provided the tools to maneuver well in a place such as New York City. There is a unique advantage to someone from an urban area who educates themselves to succeed. They have the best of both worlds and that knowledge can be beneficial as they continue to build up their position, business or concept. John truly believes that a lot can be accomplished in the City of Trenton, but the backlash is monumental when you're moving forward in a sea that has massive waves to constantly push you back. This can easily be compared to swimming upstream as it is hard but not impossible. Yet, how many people do you know that want to take the swim?

The defining of an African American business owner in any city, but especially Trenton should first be outlined by the business owner. I make that statement because many people believe that I am the only person who benefits from what John and the Chamber provides. This is not the case. I just happen to be very visible in the community so the connection is more easily recognized. I don't hide my success. I've worked very hard to obtain it; and I work just as hard to maintain it. However, I don't flaunt it. I'd much rather share what I've learned and continue to assist in the development of others. Nonetheless, they must exhibit the drive and characteristics that are reflective of a sound, stable, and motivated individual or there is no need for my assistance. This desire and motivation will dictate one's results. You get out as much as you put in!

In all of his preparation, building, and grooming, he never asked for a return on his investment. There was never any talk of taking care of him on the backend. I would have expected that coming from my life in the streets, but that wasn't the case with John. His concern was me becoming the best African-American businessman in the City of Trenton that I could possibly be. It was never a quid-pro-quo relationship and that enhanced our relationship tremendously. John embodies a man of high standards and ethical principals

IN JOHN'S WORDS...

"There is no limit to Tracey's personal goals and there is no limit to what I or my circle can provide to bring that goal to fruition. The same can be applied to any business, if the business owner is willing to listen and put in the work."

"Tracey is a chaser, who reinvents himself, explores new markets, and is just as good as the next business man. Street Smart + Business = FTB2TB."

NEXT LEVEL THINKING

If you ask John what my strengths are, he will most likely tell you it's my ability to admit my deficiencies and shortcomings. Yet, I am always interested in learning what I don't know to improve my business as well as myself. My confidence increased as I began to merge these experiences together. Today, I am more committed than ever to continuing to enhance and maintain my businesses, as well as myself.

When John initially ran for Mayor of Trenton in 2005, it was primarily based on the inability to get the current Mayor to work with him on important issues that affected African Americans in the City of Trenton. John was 8 ½ years into his term as President of MTAACC before the Mayor would sit and meet with him. One would have thought that a meeting between two prominent black leaders (one representing a business perspective and the other politics) would have worked well for the overall progress in the City of Trenton. Unfortunately, a partnership was never embraced. John spoke on record at a City Council meeting stating that the current Mayor was unwilling to meet and/or embrace partnerships that could help the city. After the news went public, a meeting was eventually set.

However, nothing developed from the initial meeting or the subsequent meetings. The Mayor would arrive late and at most times seemed very uninterested or uncommitted to the dialogue or game plan that John was presenting. These actions fueled John's decision to run against him in the next election to challenge what he believed were injustices toward the residents of Trenton. At that time statistics showed the City of Trenton was doing less than 3% with local and black businesses. Despite the fact that the tunnel construction was $120 million, the Sovereign Bank Arena was $60 million, the Waterfront Park was $50 million, the new Marriott hotel was $65 million in conjunction to the school and the city budgets which were well north of $500 million. How could this be in a city with a black Mayor, a majority black city council, and a size of less than 8 square miles? How can you not question our ability to have black leaders lead?

John genuinely believed that the Mayor's inability or unwillingness to collaborate in ways that could help the city remove itself from its current standing was ammunition enough to challenge the Mayor for the seat.

This wasn't an easy decision for John to make as this would be in direct contrast to his role as President of the Chamber. As Chamber President, one must remain engaged in the political process, but from a neutral stance or perspective. A businessman is expected to do the same and with John running for office, I was in an awkward position. I could not take a neutral stance, but actually had to pick sides due to knowing what was at stake.

John did not believe he fell in line with his perception of a typical politician's character and personality, so he struggled with his decision to run for office. However his decision was solidified by his desire to help individual business owners enhance their business in the City of Trenton. There was a determination to help Trenton realize its true potential by elevating its profile, leveraging its history, and addressing the systematic challenges that place Trenton in an inferior position compared to other urban cities across the country.

So here's John with this vision, plan, and initiative to save the residents of Trenton who had no idea of who he was or what he stood for. He was recruited straight out of college and spent many years in New York City making a name for himself, and later established a successful trucking company. The affluent individuals of Trenton recognized him, but the grassroots community he was striving to make a difference for had no clue and chose not to embrace him.

John was defeated in the election, although he did well with the more financially astute community.

The individuals whose votes he needed to win didn't show up.

Yes, John comes from a working class family in North Trenton, but the inner-city voters couldn't relate to him. Those who could relate to John began to reach out to him and build relationships that could assist on the backend as it pertained to the reconditioning of the City of Trenton.

Capitol City Contracting was one of many businesses that would have benefited from John Harmon being Mayor of Trenton; again, as always there was no quid-pro-quo in our relationship. My business was not going to catapult to the next level because he would be Mayor. I had already expanded my business based on the knowledge, wisdom, and direction provided by John Harmon, the man.

Some people didn't vote for him because they thought I would benefit from it, when we all could have actually benefited from the change. That's a hard mindset to change. I still ask the question of how can we teach those who seem unreachable? Those individuals who have yet to grasp the notion that the impossible is possible?

John reminds me often of the mindset of those who still believe that even though we've witnessed the election of the first Black President of the United

States, people will tell you without a doubt that it was not progress, but a fluke.

John works from a place of helping individuals understand that this and many others achievements were not by chance. Success is not achieved through coincidence. We are a revolutionary race that may miss our own revolution. This revolution for economic development will not be Googled, stated as a Facebook status, downloaded or tweeted. I remain committed to making sure all of us won't miss it. Someone has to be present to show our children how to build something of value and prosper. Someone has to keep teaching and giving back.

One of the biggest gifts given to me under John's advisement is the necessity to give back to the community as a business owner. It is one of the key elements of a successful business. When I speak about what John provided to me, I am referring to the tools to build my own future. I utilized the tools, connected the dots and built sound and progressive businesses of my own. No one handed or gave me anything. In the process of mapping out the vision for my businesses, I was involved with the development of the vision for the Chamber and the two visions merged. I am just as involved in Chamber business as I am in Capitol City Contracting and The Phax Group because each entity represents a portion of my business as a whole.

The relationship between John and I remains sound and strong because as in any relationship, open communication is key if that relationship is to flourish. Not a day goes by that John and I don't talk. We both believe staying connected keeps us in the know and eliminates' any confusion that may arise from a lack of understanding. If there is ever uncertainty on my behalf, I raise a question and the answer is ultimately provided. We work together; fighting for the same results.

John attributes my success to remaining humble and connected. He believes that because I never forgot where I came from, the path I'm on is clearly defined and will continue to dictate my direction.

IN JOHN'S WORDS...

"Ask someone if they want to be successful, then describe to them what is involved in obtaining that success and watch them fall away from what they say they want. If you continue to do what you've always done, you will garner what you've always garnered. If you do what you are supposed to do, the principle is reciprocal."

"Understand that business doesn't stop at a local level. To understand the different levels of success, you have to travel outside of what's comfortable and take in different perspectives. That exposure broadens your understanding, your horizons, and allows you to see the globalization of business."

"We need to realize and develop a game plan ahead of time to deal with the fact that the net worth of blacks compared to whites is extraordinarily low. We need to understand that poverty will be elevated, the drop-out rate of our youth will be elevated, the incarceration rate of our young adults will be elevated, if we don't make the necessary changes now."

"Motivating Factors consist of the following:

- If success has been achieved before, it is also available for you.
- Change just doesn't happen, you have to make it happen.

Tracey realized this a long time ago. He realized he wanted to be successful; however, he had to embark on a different path to achieve sustained success. "

"In a city like Trenton, often times it's not only "the white leaders" that can hold you back...it's also the insecure blacks who do whatever it takes to maintain their prominence at the expense of others. Unfortunately, Trenton has been an underperforming city for decades, like many other urban cities across America. It has not been about the people since the Civil Rights Movement which provided the foundation for today's leaders. The irony is the poor, uneducated, and misinformed may never realize their fullest potential due to their perpetual alignment with familiarity, emotion, and self-serving leadership. These are some of the challenges we face in the future."

CHANGE IS COMING

In order for me to continue to grow as a successful leader and continue to build my businesses, I also have to align myself with the appropriate people and map out a team that would be beneficial to the growth of my business. Over the years I've made external changes and with John's assistance in connecting me with the appropriate professional people, I've recognized my growth. In order to get to the next level, as there is always a next level to reach, I have to do the same internally. Time is money and both are resources that should not be wasted.

There is a drive in me that derives from my ancestry. A commitment to excellence that I know was passed down from generation to generation, and even though I lost my way temporarily, I found my way back and I'm continuing to build the legacy that is the Syphax name. I know my father passed it on to me. I believe I have passed it on to my son and although we have all faced adversity, we have all found our way back to greatness.

CHAPTER 6
3 Apples from the Same Tree

2http://www.arlingtonblackheritage.org/exhibits/syphaxesfamily.html

Syphax, a name that dates back to royalty2, and usually initiates conversations with **"Where did you get that name from?"** I'm almost inclined to say my family lineage stems from African royalty, but I smile and without hesitation begin to explain my history. Once the chronicle ends, the listener typically stares back at me in disbelief. Almost with that look of, "Yeah okay Tracey!" Yet it is true, and I always encourage people to Google it. If they choose to, they will discover that the Syphax name goes all the way back to the days before slavery to the story of a magnificent young slave name Charles Syphax.

Charles Syphax was the son of a free black preacher and an enslaved woman who was born at the home of his mother's owners, Martha and George Washington3. The apple reference should make more sense now.

I encourage all to read the history of their family because mine has helped me to better understand my father, myself, and my son.

My father, Frank Syphax was raised by William Syphax in Washington, D.C. William wasn't a drug dealer, but it is my understanding that he did have a hustler's mentality. He was a pool shark of some sort and was well respected in the streets.

I don't know how much of an influence my grandfather William had on my father, but what I do remember about my father from my youth was that he was a no nonsense, 6-foot afro wearing man, who was quite handsome from what I could gather from the conversation the ladies would have whenever he was around. I know that he was no non-sense because although he didn't live with us and his relationship with my mother had ended, he still was the provider of my punishment. Between the ages of 9 and 11, whenever I would get into trouble, my mother would put me on a Greyhound bus on Perry Street in

3 http://www.arlingtonblackheritage.org/exhibits/syphaxesfamily.html

Trenton and send me to Asbury Park, New Jersey to be punished by my father. I don't recall the amount of time it took to get to his house, but I do recall arriving, being whooped and within an hour of my arrival, being placed on the very next bus back to Trenton. I now laugh at the thought of being transported to another part of New Jersey to get an ass-whooping from my dad. I can't honestly say that I wouldn't classify it as authoritative parenting. I say that because there was never a conversation after the ass-whooping to express the expectation of maturity that was to follow the ass-whooping. That was the extent of our relationship at that time. I got into trouble, he punished me, and I returned home.

As I developed and began battling my demons with using and selling drugs, my father was battling his own demons of becoming clean and leaving the drug user/drug dealer game behind him. However, his involvement in the dope game was never influential to me, so it's purely coincidental that I chose his side-line of work as my career path at the time. Our only common denominator in the involvement of the drug game to any degree was my mother.

Frank Syphax worked from the moment he graduated high school. He met my mother shortly before graduating. They were soon married in 1961, with the birth of me and my brother following quickly. By 1966 their marriage was over.

My father worked odd jobs after the divorce became final and he continued to hustle on the side. I'm not aware of how good or bad he was at the hustling game, but I do know that after his first and last stint in the penal system, he was ready to change his life. My redemption took a little longer.

Once released from jail he found a job with the Naval Weapon Station Earle in Colts Neck, NJ. By the 1970s he discovered a program called "Upper Mobility," where individuals would learn the necessary skills to move from a blue collar to a white-collar working environment. He jumped at the chance and they immediately sent him to San Francisco for training. He spent a year there and when he returned he approached his new wife with his decision to seek out a white-collar job in the hopes of obtaining her support and approval. This would mean less money because there would be no overtime, but like Margaret had stood by me when I decided to become my own boss, my dad's wife was supportive of his decision.

By this time I was heavy into drugs and the drug game. Every time I was incarcerated the connection with my father grew stronger, as he became much more active in my life. I believe he recognized I needed a positive role model in my life who wasn't a pimp or hustler. I needed my father.

In many ways I am grateful for my incarceration. Not only did it open my eyes and show me a better way of living, it also allowed me the opportunity to build a stronger relationship with my father.

Visits to incarcerated individuals allow for two hours of continuous communication at the minimum. I learned things about my father during those conversations that I hadn't known previously and he got to know his son. He saw my weaknesses, my flaws, and shared with me what he saw as my strengths and potential for greatness. He stated that he was proud of my progress. I was taking the first steps to changing who I had been in order to become the person I am today. He saw it.

The similarity in our development once we decided to change our life's direction is uncanny. Like my father, I turned to African American studies and during our visits we discussed the things he learned while incarcerated at great length. I never realized how militant and knowledgeable my father was of our African culture until we began to have those conversations.

Although it took a few more jail stints for me than him, once the lesson was learned, we both sought out assistance to better our situation and reach back to our sons to fix what had been broken.

So what was broken with my son? If you can imagine a boy who loves his father, but longs for his physical presence and guidance but his father is incarcerated for crimes he committed, you will have a better understanding of what was broken in my son.

Although I was there to witness his birth, I wasn't mentally connected to his development or actively involved in the nurturing of his childhood, because I was so addicted to drugs. Even though I wasn't there as I should have been, Marquis, the baby of my two children was and remains a very intelligent young man.

Our relationship, like the relationship I have with my father was more or less established from behind the prison wall. I wasn't there every night to go over homework or discuss the things that boys experience. I believe because of this, Marquis began to develop a strong resentment towards me. He'd cry when he knew he had to visit me, but once there, he'd cry when it was time to leave.

A child of an incarcerated parent has it tough, yet they also grow to understand the responsibility of having to pay for your actions. They see firsthand the results and penalties for one's actions.

The **same tree methodology** comes into play once the change in direction takes place. Like in the moments where my father began visiting me in jail after changing his life to discuss consequences of one's actions; I spoke frankly to Marquis about those same consequences while inside the penal system.

Once home from jail, with my transformation becoming more and more apparent, I continued to share those life lessons with my son. Although I'd grown to respect and honor my relationship with my father, and his opinions, I did not want to miss the mark with my son by waiting too long to discuss life and life's lessons. I wanted to prevent him from making the same mistakes that I'd made. I'm reminded of the day I had an epiphany about what I needed to do for myself, my family and ultimately my community. It was that cold October day in 1995 during the Million Man March with Marquis by my side.

So imagine my dismay when I realized he, like me and my father before me had chosen the way of the streets instead of the way of the mind. For whatever the reason of me and my father, it differed greatly from my son.

I can only assume my father hustled to supplement his income. I hustled for the income, but more so to supplement my habit. **Marquis chose the street life to belong to something other than me.**

By the time he was a teenager, I was well established in my business and successful. Many people in Trenton and surrounding areas knew who I was and recognized those red Capitol City Contracting trucks. This was hard for Marquis because the more my business grew, the more the expectation for his greatness grew. He was his father's son and the weight of following in my footsteps from a positive perspective was heavily placed upon his shoulders. In addition to that pressure, the expectation to rebel was placed upon his shoulders by his peers. It wouldn't be long before one of the two options would prevail. **He chose the streets.**

It's easy for me to want to take the blame. To place upon my shoulders his pain in order to lighten the load, but that wouldn't be beneficial to him, nor would it be completely true. I know that because I continued to talk to Marquis about the wrongs that I'd done in my life and because he'd witnessed incarceration up-close and personal, there was no excuse to justify his decision. Yet he provided me with a reason nonetheless. Marquis had convinced himself that if he couldn't be better than me, then he would ultimately be a failure. Even with friends who had come from broken homes constantly telling him how great his opportunities were for him at home, he still chose to stay in the streets.

Now at 26 years of age, my son, Marquis Syphax, the spitting image of me is completing a 3 year bid for robbery. He admits that the decision to be involved in the robbery was his own, but that he acted out of peer pressure and a strong desire to belong. I remind him that he always belonged. He belongs to one of the most influential families dating back before slavery. I remind him that the Syphaxes were considered African Royalty and it is our responsibility to honor our lineage. We have such a rich legacy, not in the monetary sense, but in the succession sense, and that wonderful legacy, courtesy of my immediate family, will continue with Marquis and his older sister Trachell.

In contrast to the decision that Marquis made, Trachell chose to make wiser decisions. These are two children, raised by the same parents, in the same household who were subject to the same upbringing, yet they chose two totally different life paths. Marquis is currently housed in a correctional institution and Trachell is currently a New Jersey Corrections Officer, and I still remain equally proud of both of my children.

Today Marquis will tell you he still desires to be **BIGGER** than me. Not in competition with me, but to take Capitol City and The Phax Group to a level I've yet to realize. He wants to be able to pass this business on to his children and states emphatically that jail has provided a sense of clarity from the streets, although voluntarily, that held him hostage.

I've told him that I didn't begin to turn my life around for the better until I was 32 and he's responded by saying he **HAS** to get it right at 26...his life depends on it. He believes as the successor to Tracey Syphax, the man he continues to be amazed by, in awe of, and having a great deal of respect for...that something has to be proven and the change has to be evident. "It is my job to carry the Syphax name in a positive light," Marquis says.

I am convinced that this last jail bid will be remembered as Marquis' hiccup and once released; he will have held his breath just long enough to have moved passed it, and return to life triumphant.

3 apples from the same tree! A magnificent tree that bore hustlers, contractors, educators, doctors, and activist alike, we are a proud bunch of individuals, rich in history.

The Syphax name is listed on several historical landmarks in Washington D.C., and Virginia. If you have a chance to visit the historical Arlington Cemetery in Virginia, stop by the slave quarters where you will see pictures and names of many of my Syphax ancestors like Charles and Maria Syphax lining the walls. I am most proud of my family's historical achievement of opening the William Syphax School, which is strategically placed within the Syphax Village.

The Syphax Village is another cultural landmark in Washington D.C. During the last 10 years the school has undergone some major renovations after being infested with drugs. It now serves as a catalyst for the neighborhood. It reminds me of my immediate family because after major renovations my father returned to be a catalyst in my life. Although I'd always had the conversation with Marquis, I didn't lead by example, so I had to be renovated and now I can truly serve as a catalyst in his life. All of our lives; my father's, my son's, and mine, were cleaned up, reborn, and reestablished after being infested by drugs.

Just as the William Syphax School thrives in Washington D.C., the decedents of William Syphax in Trenton, New Jersey do the same, and our family legacy continues.

PICTURES AND MEMORIES

Granddad, Grandmom Troy & Tracey, 1967

On the Car: Troy, Alonzo & Tracey, Miller Homes 1968

Tracey at Grant School

Troy and Tracey

91

Troy's funeral 1969

Stoplight Bid Brings 40 Cops

By Frank Herrick and Gregory Gogo
Staff Writers

The death of an eight-year-old boy yesterday sparked a potentially explosive demonstration of nearly 400 persons who blocked traffic on Lincoln Ave. and vowed not to move until a traffic light was erected.

The crowd eventually was promised a policeman would be stationed at the hazardous intersection and the city would do all it could to get the light.

However, more than six hours later, a few dozen demonstrators remained at the scene, saying they would stay the night.

For the most part peaceful, the situation grew tense at times. A reporter was hit on the head with a brown bottle, a photographer was almost struck with a broken brick and a passing car was damaged by tossed rocks.

The boy, Troy Dume Syphax, son of Mr. and Mrs. Frank Syphax of the Miller Homes, 182 Monmouth St., was struck and killed by a truck at Lincoln and Seward Aves. at 8:15 a.m. yesterday.

The demonstrators moved into the street at 4 p.m. blocking all traffic coming from Perry and Olden and Stuts and Chambers, creating a massive traffic jam.

Some 40 policemen moved into the area but did not attempt to disperse the crowd. Officers spoke with the demonstrators in an attempt to get them to move to the sidewalks, but they refused.

The crowd demanded that Mayor Carmen J. Armenti, Council President Peter W. Radio Jr. and Public Safety Director John Heffin come to the intersection to hear their demands.

Heffin reached the scene at 5 p.m. and started to address the crowd from a public address system of one of the police cruisers.

(Continued on Page 47)

PROTEST — A crowd of approximately 400 persons blocked traffic yesterday on Lincoln Ave. and threatened to stay until a traffic light was installed at Seward Ave. (Another Story on Page Five).

DEMONSTRATION — Police Chief John A. Lanahan, center, left photo, and Capt. John McKeever discuss demands of 400 demonstrators with Walter (Pinky) Brown, right, on Lincoln Ave. yesterday. In the other picture, a demonstrator restrains the mother of eight-year-old Troy Syphax as she displays a newspaper containing the story of her son's death.

Toi, Mom, Tracey & Dad, Graduation 1979

Claitt's Bar

Debbie, Tracey & Margaret
at Puppy Dog's New Year's Eve 1977

Tracey & Margaret Don Q's Night Club

RIVERFRONT & YARDVILLE

BACK IN THE DAY

Tracey's Bachelor Party

Mitch, Tony, Tracey, Byron, Cliff, Troy & Mark

BT's Lounge

Smitty, Tracey, Fish, Dollar & Blue

Margaret, Tracey, & Trachell

Tracey & Margaret receiving the historical award for the rehabilitation of 740 West State Street Trenton, NJ

Tracey giving his 1st commencement speech to the Titusville Academy

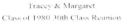

Tracey & Margaret Class of 1980 30th Class Reunion

Our Wedding Day 1985

96

Tracey & Marquis

Sanaa

Brooklyn

TRACEY D. SYPHAX

Gregory "Shoes" Marshall, Frank Syphax & Tracey

Margaret, Tracey, Former Mayor Doug Palmer,
Louise Shabazz, Councilwoman Lartigue & Trachell

Siblings: Tracey, Frank Jr., Nisey, Tyrone & Mark

Tracey, Sommore & Councilman Pintella

Tracey, Danny Glover & Margaret

Former Mayor David Dinkins and Tracey

MOB Crew
Dr. Hernandez, Margaret
Tracey
Kevin Wortham
and
John Harmon

Former Mayor Doug Palmer, Chuck Smith
Senator Hillary Clinton, Tracey, Jocelyn White
& John Harmon

Tracey & Former Governor Christie Whitman
Tracey was the recipient of the City News
Competitive Inner City Award

Tracey & Rutgers Basketball Coach, Vivian Singer

Tracey & New Orleans Former Mayor Ray Nagin

Tracey & Journalist Steven Smith

Tracey & New Jersey Lt. Governor,
Kim Gudadagno

99

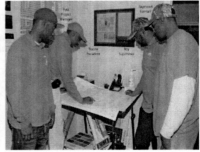

HISTORICAL REHAB 740 WEST STATE STREET
TRENTON, NEW JERSEY

AWARD WINNING REHABILITATION

TRACEY D. SYPHAX

909 BELLEVUE AVUENUE, TRENTON NJ

TRENTON HISTORICAL BEST INFILL AWARD

CHAPTER 7
Life Support~ Margaret's Perspective

"Once we learn each other and know each other's
ways…we will dance"

36 years…yes, that is a very long time to be with the same person, but it tells the story of how strong the love is between me and my husband.

It all started in the 8th grade, but I really didn't begin to pay close attention to him until I was in the 9th grade on hall patrol. There I was, stationed near his locker with my orange safety belt across my chest and my safety patrol badge. I would throw up my hands to stop him in the hall and he would always have to say something to me. When I wasn't in school, I was at the Westward Recreational Center in West Trenton hanging out with friends. It wasn't long before Tracey started to come around. One day he asked if he could walk me home and I said yes. We were 13 years old; even though Tracey lied and said he was 15 at the time. He lied because I told him I didn't date boys my own age. I don't know why I told him that, but I did. After walking me home that first day, we were instantly an item and he would come to my house early every morning to walk me to school.

We'd walk to school together and we would rest on the retaining wall that enclosed the biggest black oak tree in Mercer County. The tree was directly in front of 909 Bellevue Avenue in Trenton, NJ. Coincidently, this same location would eventually become the place we would build our dream home.

After school, Tracey would stay at my house until about 11pm. He'd call me when he got home and we'd eventually fall asleep on the phone. We were always together. I even learned to write like him so I could do his homework, while we studied at the house each night. It was true puppy love at its best.

Tracey was boxing when I met him and continued to box for a little more than a year after we started dating. I don't remember him being the greatest boxer, but he was pretty good. It didn't matter if he was the worst boxer in the world, I was going to be there cheering him on and being supportive. Tracey was always the quiet type and didn't really like drama. People often perceived his demeanor to that of a punk, but he was far from that. He didn't go looking for trouble, but he wasn't about to let you bring trouble to his doorstep either.

By the time Tracey was 16 and selling drugs I knew nothing about it. He actually did a really good job of hiding his drug dealing life from me. I knew he worked at the bar using doctored documents, so I assumed that's where his money came from.

Soon we were entering Trenton Central High School together, and I hated it. Not the part about us entering high school together, but the high school itself. It was so different than junior high school. There was so much drama and most of it stemmed from girls wanting to get with Tracey. Girls would call and threaten me because they wanted to be with him. All I wanted to do was graduate and get out of there.

Tracey was incarcerated by the time graduation rolled around. That meant there would be no prom and we wouldn't be celebrating our graduation together. I can't say I was angry about it, I was just happy that the high school experience was over.

In the blink of an eye, we were 18 years old and Tracey's drug activities were no longer a secret to me. Gone were the days of blaming his misfortune on others, as it was very obvious to me by then. He wasn't just a drug dealer, he was a drug user, and I still loved him.

By the time he was heading to Yardville Youth Reception & Correctional Center, I had a decision to make. Do I continue to communicate and complete a two-year jail bid with this man? Was my love strong enough to overcome the stress and loneliness that comes from dating a man in jail? I didn't know. All I knew was my love for him was stronger than anything I'd ever experienced, so we did the time together and eventually he came home.

Once home, he was clean and no longer sold drugs and that was good enough for me. We got engaged and I was soon pregnant. I was so excited! We were living the life we always said we wanted. We were happy! By the time our daughter Trachell was four months, I was one month pregnant with our son Marquis. No, we weren't wasting time and I wasn't going to be a mother of two children and not be this man's wife. I felt like if I was good enough to bear his children, I was good enough to marry!

We were married in front of 300 guests at Friendship Baptist Church on August 24, 1985. Our reception was at the War Memorial Building in Trenton and I just remember it being one big beautiful party. It was the most memorable day of my life. I felt absolutely beautiful as I sat in my hotel room having my make-up applied at the Holiday Inn that once sat on the corner of Calhoun and West State Streets in Trenton. I slipped into my white wedding dress and prepared to take my vows in front of God and place my life in Tracey's hands. At that moment I thought to myself, "I knew I was going to marry this man one day." I think I knew from the moment I laid eyes on him that it would be me and him against the world.

Although he was never fond of Tracey, my father walked me down the aisle. He did not want me to marry him and would do an impression of shaking jail bars whenever he would discuss Tracey with me. I really wish he would have had the opportunity to know the man that Tracey is today. He would be so proud of his son-in-law. I can only hope that he's looking down in admiration as I sometimes catch myself doing when I look at my husband.

By 1986, we were married with two children. Tracey was Foreman on his job and we were doing alright. We moved the family from our apartment to my father's house for logistical purposes. It was easier for me to get back and forth to work and my sister had agreed to babysit the kids for us. Tracey was traveling a lot and I had no idea of his indiscretions while he was on the road with his crew. However, after a few months of traveling and being on the road, he began to demonstrate his past behaviors and I was no longer interested in that lifestyle. I had been willing to turn a blinds eye as his girlfriend in the past, but not as his wife and the mother of his two children. **WE TOOK A BREAK...**

This wasn't a short break by any means. Tracey was back in the hustle game in full force. Thinking that we would not reconcile our relationship, I began dating. I encountered successful, intelligent men whose desires were to take care of me and my children. It was a very different time in my life because I'd only loved one man since I was 13 years old. Now, after marrying him and birthing his babies, I was single again... but technically still married. Tracey was dating Sherry and I was well aware of their relationship. There weren't any ill feelings towards her because the life that Tracey and I shared was over. At least for the moment it was.

Tracey would come to the door requesting to see the kids at odd hours of the night, when he knew the children would be sleeping. It seemed at times that it is much easier for a man to do what he wants to do, than to watch or allow his spouse to do the same. However, that wasn't my concern. Tracey had chosen the street life over our family life and I'd chosen to walk away.

THEN HE GOT SHOT!

I had a dream one night that Tracey had gotten shot. I called him and shared my nightmare with him as I felt it pertinent based on his current lifestyle. He ignored my concerns and disregarded my fears and two days later, he was lying in the street from a gunshot wound and I was receiving a phone call informing me that my husband had been shot. Coincidence?

I was in Newark at the time of the call. I can't even remember who called me. I just remember being frozen in time for a moment. I couldn't feel my face to even know if I was crying. It felt like I was having an outer body experience. Everything about our lives flashed before me and I needed to be where he was. I wasn't absolutely sure about what happened, and I didn't care. I just needed to be there. I jumped in the car with a co-worker and he drove me back to Trenton. I felt like I could have run alongside the car and gotten there faster. It seemed to take forever to get to Trenton. I needed to get to that hospital, to tell him things, to fix us before we couldn't! I couldn't imagine him dying and not knowing even though we weren't together I still loved him very much.

When I finally arrived I walked to the back and the doctors told me about the exploratory surgery that needed to be done. The bullet had traveled through his arm, to his stomach and was now lodged in his back 1/8 of an inch away from his spine. He'd lost a lot of blood and I was slightly offended that they wanted to discuss the price of blood instead of focusing on replacing what he'd lost. As if I would have said, "Oh no that's too much, don't save my husband's life!" They let me see him before they took him in for surgery. As I looked down at him, tears began to run down my face. I told him he was going to be okay and that I would be there when he got out of surgery. I didn't know where Sherry was at the time. Honestly, I didn't have time to concern myself with that element of his life. He was apologizing for the pain he'd caused me and all of his past indiscretions. Yes, it was very necessary to get it all out in the open since we honestly had no idea if this would be the last time we'd get to say what we truly felt to one another. I told him it was okay as I stroked his hands and face. I kept telling him it was all going to be okay, and then they took him into surgery.

It seemed like surgery took an eternity, but it was really more like 3 hours. His father stayed in the waiting room with me. I honestly don't recall where his mother was, but she wasn't there. As I sat there all I could recall was the dream I'd had two days prior. I sat there quiet, motionless, and unable to cry or show emotion. The doctor came out and told us the surgery went well and that he was in recovery. They placed him in a drug induced coma because of his addiction to heroin. They had to keep him in the coma to manage his pain and his withdrawal symptoms. When they tried to bring him out of the coma, Tracey was uncontrollable and tried to remove the respirator. He needed the respirator to live, so they placed him back in a coma for about 3 weeks. I remember my mother buying him a radio because she believed the music would soothe him while he was in the coma. She knows she loves herself some Tracey.

When they finally took him out of the coma, it didn't take him long to sign himself out of the hospital. They called me, but by the time I arrived he was standing outside in his hospital gown, ass out! I had no choice but to take him home. Tracey was at my house no longer than 3 hours and then he was gone. He was gone and instantly we were pretty much back to where we were before he'd gotten shot. After everything we'd said in the hospital, all of the apologies and begged forgiveness were now out the window. God had allowed him to live and he showed his appreciation by returning to the streets. I didn't have the energy to deal with it, so I just accepted his decision. Not long after him leaving my home did I hear about him bailing Sherry out of jail and that they were back in business.

HE GOES BACK TO JAIL

This time around I had no interest in visiting or making it a normal activity in my children's life. I mean how many times were we going to relive this process? I didn't want to strip my children of their father completely, but I was exhausted with the whole jail aspect of his life. I was working and my life, as well as my children's was good.

My friend Keith owned Carter's liquor store on the corner of Hoffman Avenue and Oakland Street near Roger Gardens in Trenton. He would ask me to help him out from time to time if he was short staffed. I mostly helped on Saturdays to combat the weekend rush. One particular Saturday a few weeks after

Halloween there was a show at the Spectrum in Philadelphia and two of his employees called out to attend the show. I came right over of course to help due to the staff shortage. It was business as usual and Keith ran to Amefikas to get us something to eat. Amefikas, a Muslim restaurant on Stuyvesant Avenue in Trenton, remains a pillar in the African American community of Trenton. They have the best sweet wheat rolls on the East Coast.

When he returned, I went to the back to eat first since business was slow. We would trade places once I finished. As I walked from the back, still chewing on my sweet wheat roll, a man entered the store wearing a ball cap and bandana over the bottom half of his face. I seriously assumed that he was playing some kind of game and his attire was a left over Halloween costume. Keith kept saying, "Stop playing cousin," so seriously it never dawned on us that this guy was coming to rob the place until he raised the gun in the air. Next thing you know bullets are flying and glass is shattering as he's taking aim at every refrigerator behind the counter. I was standing right next to the silent alarm, but I couldn't move. I froze in fear and disbelief. When I was finally able to make my body move, all I could do was drop to the floor and take cover. Bullets were still flying! The one customer we had in the store had been shot, and without me even noticing two bullets had come through the counter and hit me. Keith had run to the back to retrieve his gun and the guy panicked and ran out of the store.

Keith was screaming at me to get up and run! Still in panic mode, I conjured up enough energy to run to the back. Once there I noticed that my pants were wet, but I seriously thought I'd soiled myself from fear. However, my knee and my arm were on fire. I looked down and felt my leg with my fingers. As I turned my hand over, my fingers were wet and red with my blood. I looked at Keith and screamed, "Call the ambulance, I've been shot!"

When the ambulance arrived the paramedics took a look at my wounds. The gunshot to my arm sliced my arm down to the white meat. It was a little deeper than a graze, but hadn't quite penetrated my arm. The gunshot wound to my knee had actually entered my knee, but because the bullet was slowed down by the drawer, the impact wasn't as severe as it could have been. The moment I stood up to run to the back, the bullet fell onto the floor. I was beyond lucky, but I was in severe shock. They took me to the hospital, but I wouldn't stay. I'd watched one too many movies where the killer came back to finish the job, fearful that the victim would be able to identify him. He wouldn't have to worry about me because I wouldn't be there when he came to finish the job. I was also hoping that he didn't know me personally.

After that incident I was scared and immediately felt the need to have a strong male figure in my presence. My father had retired to Florida and Tracey was in jail. Tracey was having a fit because he couldn't be there to protect me and alleviate my fears. I think more than any other time he'd been incarcerated, this time he regretted the actions that placed him behind that jail wall. He fought with feelings of responsibility because he wasn't there to protect me and our babies. He struggled with the question of whether or not I would have even been working there and gotten shot had he been home. These were questions we didn't have the answers to, but I knew that I really longed for my husband after that incident.

His normal calls of twice a week became more frequent and this allowed for our communication to increase. We discussed our marriage, the bad decisions he'd made, and what we needed to do to get our lives back on track. We decided we were going to get back together. I told him the communication with Sherry would need to stop immediately. Although I held no grudges because they were together when we were technically separated, I was back and that meant she would have to be a thing of the past. He agreed and we began to pick up the pieces.

By the time Tracey was released from the halfway house I had purchased a condominium on Southard Street in Trenton. We were starting over and I believed wholeheartedly that the drug portion of his life was behind him. What I couldn't believe was that the location of our new home was directly in front of the spot where he once laid from a gunshot wound years before. I never knew where on Southard Street he laid, possibly taking in his last breath until the first time he arrived at our doorstep. It must have been surreal for him to walk outside and see that spot every day. I don't think that's something one would easily forget.

Everything was good. He was drug free and we were both working. It all looked as if it were going to fall apart after going out with friends one night. He was home by the time I returned and it was obvious to me that he was high. I had no intention of arguing or fighting, but I did have every intention of getting him out of my children's home because I was NOT going to have an addict living around my children. They were bigger, more impressionable, and it was obvious to me that he **WAS NOT** ready.

I told him that I was going to pack me and the kid's clothes and go to my mother's house for a few days. I instructed him that when I returned he was not to be there. He pleaded with me to forgive him. He said he was merely obliging his friends in engaging in a quick hit, and I reminded him that he should have been obliged to do right by his wife and kids, not his fake friends. Friends do not encourage their friends to get high! Especially after witnessing everything that drugs had taken from that friend's life.

I didn't need Tracey...I loved Tracey! Yet, I did not love him more than my children or myself. I didn't need his drug drama, nor was I interested in his empty promises. There were men who would have loved to take his place! I am a good woman! I looked my husband in the eye and I asked him, matter-of-factly, **"Do you want this marriage to work?"** He firmly stated yes and we have not had an issue with drugs again to this day.

By April of 1996 I started working for the Department of Corrections. Tracey was working a regular 9 to 5 roofing job and was making really good money. This was also around the time he was laying the foundation for Capitol City Contracting. He was paying all of the bills; we'd placed both kids in Catholic school, and were saving money so that we could purchase a larger home. Between the 9 to 5 job and the Capitol City Contracting business he was putting in 16 hour days, and working 7 days a week for a little over a year. He was killing himself! Although I know he had something to prove to himself, I couldn't sit by and watch him work himself into a grave. I'd finally gotten the husband I'd always wanted and deserved and I wasn't going to let a job take him away from me. I told him to make a choice. Shit or get off the pot! Either way, something was getting flushed because we were not going to allow anything to slow us down.

The closer we got to our dream of owning our new home, a home we'd build from the ground up, the more I watched my husband come into his own. The house was his baby. Growing up Tracey never had a home to call his own. They always lived in an apartment or rented a room from a family member. This was his dream and I supported him in it. I'll always support my husband in his dreams. We may not always agree on how to get there, but I was, and will always remain the biggest supporter of his dreams.

I remember us driving to the lot that would hold our future home. We stood beneath the simple frame of the structure and discussed how far we'd come. This was the same lot that housed that big black oak tree that we once rested upon during our walks from junior high school. This was the same location where countless conversations were held about our future life on our walks home from school. Words can't express how grateful we were to be there at that moment. Tracey had Pastor Simeon Spencer of Union Baptist Church come over and bless the ground before the house was completed. He asked the Pastor to bless it again when it was finally finished. It wasn't my dream to have that house, but it was my wish to give my children what I experienced growing up. A family with both parents in the home; and a backyard big enough for friends to come hang out. We wanted to share our family's life and love.

"Once we learn each other and know each other's ways... we will dance"

That line reminds me of standing beneath the frame of that house, a mere shell of what was to come. We danced beneath that beautiful night sky with stars twinkling above us. I love my husband more than words can express. I still see that 13 year old boy who lied and said he was 15. I still remember not wanting to be away from him longer than to sleep and wake up to and find him standing in my kitchen ready to walk me to school. I remember the tears in his eyes as he lay in that hospital bed and the look of regret and sorrow when he left after only being able to stay in that house with me for three hours because those drugs were calling his name. And after everything...after all of that, I still want to grow old in his arms and I will, assisting and supporting him whenever times get hard.

We thought the hard part was over. We built the house, Tracey's businesses are successful, our children were coming into their own, and we had a wonderful relationship with God. That was the case for more than eight years and then the Christmas of 2010 everything changed.

Tracey began experiencing extreme back pain in July of 2010. Unaware of the cause, he made an appointment and the doctors ran a few routine test. The test results showed a high PSA count, which is a sign of cancer. This was cause for alarm because Tracey's father Frank had been diagnosed with prostate cancer. The doctors decided to run additional test, which went on for several months. We were optimistic, and Tracey was very at ease with whatever the outcome would be. He explained to me that he was far removed from the drug culture where he'd spent 16 years and that he now believed his life had balance, and whatever God had decided for him was okay with him.

It was two days before Christmas, and we were riding to the Cancer Institute of New Jersey in New Brunswick. I remained quiet for the majority of the drive, while Tracey blasted rap music, which included Biggie Smalls. I do recall asking him to please turn it down.

We arrived at the Institute and they called us into the Consultation room. It felt like it took forever for the doctor to come in and speak with us. Once the doctor entered the room he pulled out his chart. There was a pause, which somewhat foretold the negative prognosis. **Tracey had cancer!**

He explained the three treatment options. One was to monitor it and hope that it would spread

119

slowly. The other option was radiation treatment, which could result in the cancer coming back in 4-5 years and they would be unable to operate. The third option was for Tracey to have emergency surgery within 90 days because his prostate was 60% cancerous.

We were unable to process this information immediately. We sat there numb with blank stares. I asked several questions about the options he laid out and Tracey informed me that we would seek a second opinion before moving forward with any decision.

We returned to the car and I had a thousand thoughts swimming in my head. I asked Tracey how he felt about the prognosis and once again he said he was fine with whatever God had in store for him. I gazed out the window and Tracey once again cranked up the rap music. He went from Biggie to Tupac.

When I got home I spoke to my mother about it. She was the only one who knew besides me and Tracey. Christmas morning the family was joyous as always; with our grandbaby Brooklyn running around, our nieces and nephews choosing their designated dining spots around the dinner table, and Tracey and I keeping the secret we learned only two days prior.

Tracey is always tasked with blessing the food during the holidays. Just as Tracey began blessing the

120

food, my mother started to weep. As everyone raised their heads and realized she was crying, Tracey and I knew we had to share the news with the family. I looked at Tracey, he nodded, and I came and stood by his side as he told the family that he had cancer. The mood wasn't as somber as I expected it to be because of the way Tracey shared the prognosis with them. It was almost as if he had put them at ease with what he had so eloquently come to terms with.

The surgery which had a 93% success rate was scheduled for the third week of March 2011. It lasted several hours and I was waiting in Tracey's room with my mother, Trachell and Brooklyn's father, Pete Lewis. He was still a little groggy when he came in the room and I tried to console Trachell and Pete who were softly crying.

I brought Tracey home a few days after the surgery and reminded him that he was to rest for at least three months. It lasted all of two weeks. He was right back to work and running his businesses as usual.

That's just the nature of my husband. He's always working and building his brand.

After everything, I felt as if the cancer brought us closer. We once again overcame a hurdle, unified in our efforts to beat the odds. Not just cancer, but in life. I'm sure this had everything to do with the little conversation I had with my God about us. I simply requested a little more time because I truly believed we weren't quite through yet.

When I look at my husband today I am in awe of his accomplishments. I appreciate him deeply and I am very much in love with him **STILL**. We talk to one another. We're honest with one another, and our communication is clear. It has to be. If I'm unhappy I have to express that to him so we can find a way to fix it and it works the exact same way in reverse. He has to tell me what's missing so that we can get things back in order.

A marriage is a commitment and often times people walk away from it because of circumstances that could have easily been rectified. If I had to share the secret to our 36 years of togetherness, I'd say we didn't dwell on or count the breaks. Our bond is stronger today than it ever was because we put GOD first, our family second, and everything else just fell into place. If I was to share anything with people it would be to keep outsiders out of their business. To my women friends I'd say stop letting outside forces dictate your relationship. When problems arise in your relationship, talk it out first with **YOUR MATE!** The relationship is between the two of you and so it is recommended that the two of you work through your differences together, and that will keep you two from falling apart.

When asked what my definition of LOVE is, I reply softly by stating my husband's name. I say it with a smile and a sense of warmth flushes over me, and spiritually I'm right with the world. Tracey doesn't complete me, he compliments me and the picture is beautifully in focus.

Love is trust, honesty, being able to forgive, and it's a bond that honestly no-one other than God himself can come between. It's magnetic. It is so strong, that when that person is gone too long you wish for them to return. However, in your heart they never leave.

I find myself at times staring at this man who has been through so many things in his life...the good, the bad, the ugly, and the extreme, and whispering softly as if he can hear me, **"I've always seen the good in you."**

At events when I'm sitting in my picture perfect dress, beautifully presented as the extension to this wonderful man, I look over at him in his tailored suit conducting business, bars removed and I am full with emotion. **I'm proud of him.** I know his life, his struggles, his journey, and the many obstacles he's conquered or overcome. He says I am his rock...I know he is my inspiration, and my first and only true love.

CHAPTER 8
THE BLUEPRINT

By definition, a blueprint is a detailed outline or plan of action. Throughout this entire book I've discussed the obstacles, struggles, and triumphs that have allowed me to get to this point in my life. I've shared information with you about business operations in Chapter 5 that would begin to prepare you in operating your own business. Now I'm going to take it one step further and give you **"THE BLUEPRINT."**

Will what I am about to share with you make you rich beyond your wildest imagination? I cannot guarantee such a thing, but I will say if you follow the simple outline I provide, put in the hard work necessary for you to accomplish what needs to be accomplished, then you will become rich by any standards, even if that doesn't come in a monetary form. I only ask that you take the information I share with you and develop and grow your business accordingly. If you aren't interested in the entrepreneurial path, I hope the blueprint at least provides you with an outline to build your own brand of work ethic within the organization you are currently employed. I hope it empowers you to expand your world both in business and in life.

SO LET'S GET STARTED

The first thing you need to do is instill a sense of confidence in yourself. You will need to begin to believe that you have the ability to change your life's circumstance. Your situation is not your destination. If you currently aren't happy with the way your life is playing out, stop and ask yourself first how you can change your life's direction. Write down all the things that are currently unsatisfactory within your life and beside it write down your plan of action to overcome it.

Next, decide on your desired business. We all have things we are good at; trades and skills we've acquired, or dreams and desires we wish to pursue. So start by writing down these five words and define each. **Why, Who, When, How, and Where do you want to go?** Why are you going into this business? Who are you as it relates to others in the business you've chosen? **When** is the product or service coming to fruition? **How** are you going to get it to the market? **Where** do you want to take this business?

I'm sure you're saying that you've never written a business plan before, and wouldn't know where to begin to develop one. However, if you've written and defined the five words and questions above, you've basically done just that. Yes, you have developed a business plan. You may still wish to do more research through the internet and library, and begin to map out a more defined plan. However, you have the basic essentials necessary to get started. The rest is a just a formality.

Next I'd suggest that you reach out to individuals who've written business plans. Allow them to share with you the pitfalls they've encountered so that you may possibly avoid them. Dig deep and do your research to better understand your desired business. Pay close attention to the successes and failures of similar businesses in your vicinity. By doing this, you will begin to develop the necessary skills of researching that will prove beneficial to you as you map out your own business. There are also free classes from the Small Business Administration, a federally funded program available in cities across the U.S, as well as local small business developmental centers in your area, usually based at colleges and universities.

Now that you've established what your business is going to be and have a defined plan that will be acceptable to financial institutions, you need to find someone you can trust that knows more about business than you do. He or she doesn't necessarily have to be an expert in your field of business, but should be a successful business person.

This individual should be able to assist you in turning your dream into a reality, and act as a mentor in crafting out a lesson plan. However, you must choose wisely. You should have a list of things you expect from your mentor to ensure that he or she is suitable for the job. This is the individual who will ask you specifically what it is you wish to do from a business standpoint and based on your responses, assist you in understanding what your capabilities are, and what your next steps should be.

Sometimes all of the things we think we know are not the things we need to know.

Once you've established trust with the mentor you're ready to move forward. That trust factor will continue to confirm and build upon your **"I can do all things"** attitude. This positive connection has the ability to bring out the best in you.

So how do you define that level of trust? I would say in the same manner in which you placed trust in that drug dealer who first introduced you to the game, or the gang member who afforded you the opportunity to enter that affiliation to represent a flag. I would say in the same manner in which you love your girlfriend/boyfriend or new husband/wife, believing that they have your best interest at heart. What was it about those individuals that allowed you to trust and believe it was a beneficial move for your

127

life regardless of the consequences? Apply those same beliefs and actions to your business. Here is an opportunity to chase success where the consequence is a reward and not a penalty. This time the decision could possibly change your life for the better.

WHAT'S YOUR CAPACITY?

You've developed the business plan, you know what you need to know, and you're ready to get the business up and running. So what's your capacity? Let's say your desired business is a painting business. You've acquired a few good brushes, work clothes and work boots, and you're a hardworking and dependable individual. How do you go about soliciting business?

Keep in mind, you have turned an idea into the beginning stages of a business, but it is not a formal business. You haven't established it as such yet.

You have a few options; you can solicit business on your own to try and get the word out about your services, or you can approach an already established painting business and offer your services at no cost. Yes, you've read that correctly. I said **AT NO COST**. If you're asking yourself how this can be beneficial to your overall plan, I'll give you a fact and follow it up with an example.

The fact is, it allows people to develop an idea of who you are as an individual. By offering your services at no cost, the business owner sees that you have nothing to gain but the wealth of knowledge they have the capacity of instilling.

For example, a college student before graduating has the opportunity to take on an internship. Most internships are not funded, but provide a wealth of knowledge within the field of study of that student. This is far greater than the minimal pay he or she would receive from working in a fast food restaurant. With this training, that student will learn from the best and brightest in the business and be better prepared when entering the workforce, as an employee or entrepreneur. So this "at no cost" work you are offering to an employer is priceless to your overall goal. It's beneficial to the employer because it's free labor. It also allows for the employer to give back in the simplest fashion.

There are things you will learn about yourself during this process. A few of these things will include how well you receive and handle constructive criticism. Another will be if you have the ability to work well with others, as well as whether or not you will be able to accept and/or correct mistakes you've made on a job site. Sometimes these mistakes will come at a cost to you personally and professionally.

Why is this beneficial to your business? In your business all customers will not be satisfied with your service. That's constructive criticism that may not always come across as constructive. You'll have to find a way to correct the error and make that consumer happy. Being able to do so relates back to your ability to work well with others and learn from mistakes, at a cost to you. You're working with that customer to assure that the service they expect is parallel to the level of service you wish to consistently provide. For those of you who come from a street hustler background, this is going to be hard to do. You're used to telling people what to do, and now you're going to be told. It will be a hell of a hard transition for you to make. **HOWEVER, IT IS A TRANSITION THAT MUST BE MADE.**

One more thing to remember, although you're not getting paid, you will be expected to behave like employees who are being paid. That means if you're scheduled to be there at 8 a.m. you arrive before or by 8 a.m. If you've been scheduled to work Monday through Friday, you show up for work at 8AM Monday through Friday. **"IF YOU CAN'T BE ON TIME, BE EARLY!"** Telling you not to return to the worksite or office is not a hard task for an employer who technically isn't your employer. Keeping the internship is probably more difficult than obtaining it if you're not going to take it seriously. Ask yourself how committed you are to reaching your goal before you take this step.

How long does this **"at no cost"** process last? This is totally up to you, your ability to absorb the subject matter, and confidence to walk away from the learning process. At this phase you are still in the "worker" mode. You have not graduated to the "entrepreneur" role as yet, but you're laying the groundwork to be successful once you get there.

The free labor could possibly turn into a job based on your work performance. This will allow you to continue to learn the business you wish to establish for yourself. Ask questions, take notes and pay attention to detail. Ultimately your goal is to become as successful as the employer you now represent. So learn the business. Learn what works and what doesn't. **You have to know about a business before you can run a business!**

Whether or not you took the first option of soliciting your own clients to build your business, or the second option which I've covered in detail, you should be in a good place financially within six months to a year.

You know you've chosen the right individual to **trust and mentor you,** if he or she is assisting in mapping out the next steps in building your business. If you recognize that you made a bad choice, dissolve the relationship and seek out the assistance of someone better suited for the task.

You haven't obtained any insurance or any of the required documentation to officially be considered a business yet, as you're still very much in the tutelage phase. However, you can begin to make a few business maneuvers.

If you've been paying attention, the hope is that you have acquired a lot of knowledge about your desired business within the first 6 months to a year of implementing your business plan. You've been building your resume, taking before and after photos to showcase your work, networking and meeting the appropriate people, and taking notes about your desired business. You've become accustomed to the mindset of "Excuses are for losers" and "Failure is not an option." **You're ready for the Marketing Phase.**

HOW DO I MARKET MYSELF?

1. Network.

2. Communicate your interest.

3. Stay consistent.

4. Build and establish your brand.

5. Know your customer.

6. Know your competition and build off of their weakness.
7. Continue to research your field of business.

8. Continue to put in hard work.

9. Know the landscape.

10. Establish a standard.

First things first, you're going to need a good lawyer and a good accountant for this business. These two individuals will be beneficial to the growth and development of your business.

Know your competition! Frontwards, sideways and backwards, you must know how everyone in your field operates their business, which will affect your business. You must know their weaknesses and capitalize on them, or at the very least, learn from those weaknesses.

Keep in mind that customers will pay more if they believe they are getting more. Perception is everything. Everything about your business should be consistent and professional with a clear representation of who you are as a business owner.

Your business cannot be "**bootleg.**" It cannot be half-assed. You must give conscious thought to your business presentation at all times. When you establish a format for your business, down to something as simple as your hours of operations, you need to honor that format, **consistently.**

You need to put consistent marketing materials into place. Your signs should match your business cards. Your business cards should match your t-shirts. Your t-shirts should match your trucks, or any and all promotional material. The way your logo is positioned and colored on one item should be reflective on all items relative to your business" brand. Marketing doesn't involve a lot of steps; it involves consistent and precise messages that continue to convey the same ideology. When you see the color red and typography of the C's on a soda can, you unmistakably know it's a can of Coca-Cola. That level of visible connection should be what you reach for in your own branding.

Keep in mind that when dealing with our people the expectation to honor your format is first and foremost. Understand that blacks are more inclined to be forgiving of any other race when there are hiccups in the business format. However, we will not accept and/or make an excuse for a business owner who resembles us. Any deviation from the business owner's format results in a lack of support for their business on our behalf. This is a sad but true statement. Satisfying the customer and knowing your audience will require more than just great business acumen.

As it relates to all people, if you don't put the time into your business, your business will NOT have longevity. Successful business people are always prepared for opportunity.

HOW DO I CONTINUE TO GROW?

You grow by analyzing your process and assuring that everything within your process continues to flow smoothly. You've followed the blueprint thus far and now recognize that the blueprint is your actual business plan. You've built in areas that have allowed you to create your own specific business roadmap.

If you notice a few areas that are not allowing your business to function at is full capacity, you should ask yourself the following questions: Do you have the appropriate equipment? Are you purchasing products from the correct vendors? Are you staffed appropriately? These are just a few of several questions that you will need to ask yourself in re-evaluating your business.

You grow your business by repeating, re-tweaking and refining your process. **Why, Who, When, How, and Where do I want to go?**
Correct the areas that make your business less profitable to stay in line with the goals and objectives you defined in the beginning of the process. **Why, Who, When, How, and Where do I want to go?**

Based on your evaluation, answer the following question: **DO YOU WANT TO BE IN BINNESS OR DO YOU WANT TO BE IN BUSINESS?**

YES, there is a difference. It's the difference of settling for $1500 a week and taking two weeks off for an impromptu vacation or making $1500 a week consistently that will result in $78,000 a year.

Understand that a lot of sole proprietorships are one man or woman operations where the owner makes a net of $30 to $35K a year. If this is indeed the case, I'd ask you to consider a normal job where benefits and other options may prove more beneficial.

First and foremost, the success of your business will depend on the continual analyzing and re-evaluation of your processes, but your ability to give back to the community that embraced you is mandatory and will play a big part in whether the success of that business in that community will last. Keep in mind that business owners are held to a higher standard, and because of that, they must become the standard. Your life and actions are now watched and scrutinized by the very same people you service. You most certainly should practice what you preach and live by the same ethical and moral standards that you have outlined for your business. The loyalty of your consumer will be as good as the service that consumer receives. Let your community know you are not just there to capitalize off of their need for the service you provide, but that you are seriously connected to the community and care about the development of other businesses as well.

Ask any successful business owner what their greatest accomplishment is, and I can almost guarantee it will involve giving back to others. Success is not truly had, if not shared with others.

HOW DO YOU GIVE BACK?

One can't continue to receive with a closed hand, and once you've established yourself as a successful business person you are only as good as what you give and leave behind. How will you re-invest in your community to help others who resemble the person you once were? How will you assist the individual who never made an honest living? Will you be that someone that shows them how?

No, you can't save everyone and not everyone will be interested in being saved. However you cannot make it to the other side, which is the side where success resides and stay there. Your growth will cease and your success will be unfulfilling.

You can give back by providing information to those who wish to start their own businesses. Share with individuals the pitfalls you've experienced along the way. Make connections between individuals from different worlds who without your introduction would never have been able to hold a conversation. You can make a difference simply by recognizing a need and working with others in your community to fulfill it. It's called cooperation and collaboration.

Giving back doesn't always involve whipping out your checkbook. A person with money issues today who hasn't been properly trained on how to manage money tomorrow will continue to have money issues. No matter how much money you throw at the problem, without the proper insight, guidance and direction, the problem will remain.

You can be the business owner who allows an individual who wishes to provide free labor to learn your craft.

You can be the mentor to assist in turning someone's dream into a reality and craft out their lesson plan.

Please understand that giving back has to be a sincere gesture. It cannot be used as a ploy to obtain something in return. I can promise that what you will receive by providing guidance to someone else will be more gratifying than anything monetary. No amount of money will replace the level of satisfaction one feels when knowing they've made a difference in the life of someone Else.

So there you have it, **"THE BLUEPRINT."** The **Why, Who, When, How, and Where do you want to go?** It is the capacity, transformation, growth, marketing, financial analyzing and defining, evaluating, and deep desire to give back repeatedly that makes ordinary people, extraordinary business people.

It is you, if you so desire to follow **"THE BLUEPRINT."**

Although my contact information will be listed on the back of this book, and you are more than welcome to contact me with questions, I am almost certain that there is a Tracey Syphax in your area or your community with the knowledge and desire to help someone become their next generation's success story. Find out who they are and simply ask them if they have time to answer a few questions over a cup of coffee. You just might be surprised at how many people will be willing to help, yet they have never been given the opportunity to do so.

CHAPTER 9
WHAT'S NEXT?

The book is almost complete, and I am almost consumed with the political agenda of my city. I say almost, because I still have multiple businesses that need to be run. I love Trenton. I really do. It's the capital of New Jersey and I love it because it is a constant reminder of who I am and how far I've come. It keeps me grounded, motivated, determined, and lately...it's been keeping me up at night.

You see I'm fearful for the people in my city. I'm fearful of the city's direction, lack of community awareness, and the lingering sense of hopelessness that drapes over us like a gray cloud. The only difference is we don't have to wait for the storm, as we are standing in the midst of it.

I find hope in knowing that at the very other end of the spectrum lies optimism, because change, changes things.

I've come to understand that not everyone embraces change. As I stated previously, faith and fear can't operate in the same place at the same time. People tend to let traditions and "the way we've always done it," dictate their current decisions. They somehow are unable to move forward without being held back by their inability to view things differently and seek a resolution. When it's necessary to be in an uproar, I find that most people prefer to be quiet.

When I pull into the driveway of my office on Martin Luther King Blvd in the wee hours of the morning, the city is still. Depending on what time of the year it is, the sun is just rising over the Infamous 682 block that sits adjacent to my office building. Poppie hasn't opened his corner store yet, and people have yet to fall out of their front door to begin their trek to work. It's quiet, but my city's not peaceful. Shootings and gangs plague our city, just as they do many other urban cities, and the citizens are waiting for the **"Great White Hope"** to rescue them from their world of despair. There was a time when I would have dreaded being the individual faced with the task to tell them he doesn't exist. However, today I'd stand on any block within this 7.65 mile radius and scream that it's time for them to wake up.

Our communities are ours. The people we elect into political office to govern and oversee the progress of our communities must be held accountable by us. Yet, what I've come to know as fact is that within the community itself, we have inherited some deeply rooted obstacles that we must overcome before we can progressively move forward. Most of these obstacles are based purely on emotion.

142

Yet, no one is being held to a moral standard. **What exactly is "THE BLUEPRINT" for our community?**

Any community's possibilities are limitless if they follow a systematic blueprint that has been established for that community. Homeowners and hardworking people in every city pay local and state taxes. Those taxes serve as their investment in the city within their specific state. How do they get a return on their investment? Why is no one asking that question?

Leadership in communities across America are perpetuated, established and/or elected to office on the basis of "**NO RETURN**." The citizens can expect no return on their investment!

I want to bring attention to those who get in the door and close the door behind them. Those individuals who sell us dreams to get into office and then forget we exist once the election is over. I recognize that it is our vote that gets them in. My job now is to convince others of the same. We provide the votes, monetary supporters provide the backing. The politicians in return back the monetary supporters and their needs when they're-elected, leaving us on the outside trying to break the glass to get it.

Leaders, by design are supposed to look at a situation and decide how the people will be affected both positively and negatively. We need servant leaders not self-serving leaders. We need those who take information and make sound judgments in the best interest of the city's citizens. So why does that not happen? Why when it doesn't happen, do we not fight for our rights to change things? This is **OUR** business.

People continue to come to me and tell me that I'm too close to this political machine. They remind me that I'm too connected to a system that can ultimately destroy a businessman. The sentiment I share is always the same, "I'm a Trentonian first!" My business is where it is today strongly due to the support I received from my community. It is only right that I fight beside those who supported me through the struggles of my early years. Now that my city is currently within the pulls of its own struggle and we're not winning, here I stand.

I speak so passionately about **"THE BLUEPRINT,"** because **"THE BLUEPRINT"** establishes goals, sets objectives, holds folks accountable and has absolutely NOTHING to do with emotion. Yet, as I previously stated, as of late, politics seem to have become a pissing contest to see who can wiz the furthest and honestly it's embarrassing.

In communities where politics flow smoothly, both parties, Republican and Democrats are being held to a standard. Both parties are accountable to **"THE BLUEPRINT"** in their communities. Their work is measureable. It saddens me to say that in Trenton the bar has been lowered. On July 20, 2010 we lowered the bar even lower!

Riding through the City of Trenton you would have no idea that it is a multi-million dollar a year operation. Millions of dollars a year and someone lay shot in the street almost every week! How is that even feasible?

We need to learn that politicians work for us! We are their customers. We're investing in their brand and paying into a system that is supposed to provide garbage pickup, public safety, education and quality of life for our children. Yet we as citizens continue to be taken advantage of because we are too ignorant to the ways of a governing institution. A lot of us are satisfied with hugs and photo ops verses something tangible and real.

I'm a business man. I don't pretend to be a politician, but I now understand politics. It's imperative to the success of my business that I understand politics. I need to understand how the game is played, yet I'm angered that we're playing games with the future of our community and lives of our children. People will say, "Well Tracey's granddaughter doesn't even go to Trenton Public Schools!" I will respond, she doesn't, but I still pay into the system through my real estate taxes and I demand accountability and a return on my investment. This is expected, be it my granddaughter or any other child in the City of Trenton. So yes, I will stand on the frontline with them and fight for their just reward. Although they may not have the monetary means to send their children to private schools, their children deserve the best education possible. It's rightfully theirs and it's due.

So let's relate what I'm saying to the business element of my life. If I weren't running my business accordingly and you were a shareholder who invested in my company, it would be your right to vote to have me removed from my seat. If it would be in the best interest of the company to remove me from power, and all of the shareholders agree...I would be out of a job. If it can happen to Steve Jobs at Apple, why is it so difficult to wrap our minds around the removal of any individual who is clearly pilfering the future of children in the City of Trenton or any other urban city? We need to understand that politics is big business.

What we so desperately need are more citizens in urban cities who understand metrics, goals, and objectives. We need individuals who want to interface with leaders who can continue to define those metrics and bring about understanding and outcomes for those goals and objectives. What we don't need is a watered-down approach, in an attempt to keep people down because they are too ignorant to rise up. When will the goal be to uplift our people? As of

2011, there are more than 500 black mayors across the United States and we're still screaming about inequality!

We need to create a community filled with **BLUEPRINT** certified people, so they can begin to transform that community and reject emotional leadership. Emotional leadership perpetuates our community's ignorance, crime and breeds marginal success. Ask yourself the question of whether you've ever truly witnessed true success. Outside of Oprah and whatever else you see on television, how do you define success?

True success is strong leadership, and it is not emotional. I've stated it several times because I'm driving home the fact that leadership **CANNOT** be emotionally driven. The political and church leaders in conjunction with the community activist are the ones who keep leadership emotional. You will never hear them speaking of **"THE BLUEPRINT,"** as a standard, metric, or measurable means. You will never hear them mention it because it does not work for their success model.

The question then becomes, "How do you strategically plan to get individuals where they need to be?" How do we individualize the process with an initial assessment that allows for both a personal and **TRUE** message to each individual in the community?

People can't hide from the truth. The truth is universal.

Any successful business person will tell you that it is imperative that you first have a mission and vision statement established when starting a business. That's strategic planning. You have to answer the question of what exactly is your goal and where exactly you plan on going before you can say with affirmation, "**I HAVE A BUSINESS!**"

To better understand where our city or any other city is going direction needs to be clearly defined to make that city competitive. An agenda that's directed more towards the people of this city should be clearly communicated. The city must challenge its citizens to do better. At the same token, the city leadership must do better by its citizens. They must set the standard.

A prime example of setting the standard and a city doing better by its citizens would be reflective of the term of Atlanta's first black mayor, Mayor Maynard Jackson. He laid the **BLUEPRINT** and then followed it for the city of Atlanta starting in 1973, and in 2011 Atlanta is still reaping the benefits of his endeavors. 4Under the direction of Mayor Jackson, minority owned businesses prospered because of the programs implemented which guaranteed large shares of city contracts.

4http://www.blackseek.com/bh/2001/07_ManyardJackson.htm

I'll make the comparison to Mayor Jackson in my city, and you can compare his **BLUEPRINT** to your city.

In my city under the direction of the former Mayor, as it relates to contracts with minority- owned businesses, we missed the mark and missed the opportunity to set the **BLUEPRINT** as outlined in Chapter 5. Fast forward to 2011 and once again we've missed the mark with a $100 million dollar opportunity to redevelop Miller Homes. This Miller Homes project would have kept $30 million dollars in the city for local and minority business and could have been the current Mayor's "Maynard Jackson" moment.

After countless City Council meetings, the $30 million dollar demolition plan moved forward with little opposition from the citizens. This project was to award 30% of that $30 million to local and minority business. That would have resulted in $9 million dollars, yet the minorities hired included two black laborers and one black-owned security firm. The question remains on whether that $9 million dollar allotment was ever reached.

I am emotionally attached to the Miller Homes project because I grew up there and because my brother's blood stained the streets of that neighborhood. However, this is not about emotion.

I've come to understand how we as a people can become so emotionally attached to things and people that have no substance.

We should never elect a political official because he coached our son's baseball team, or feel as though we've been granted something monumental when we're handed a brick with a plaque to signify a piece of our local history. When are we going to demand our "Maynard Jackson" moment?

Today, Atlanta withstanding its own challenges is still exceedingly better off because they had and remain to have a standard. They stuck to their **BLUEPRINT.**

Trenton and all cities need clearly defined measureable goals and objectives to be held accountable to. Today many of us represent opposite ends of the spectrum working our way to the middle. Citizens in every city need to tap into their intelligence and not settle for being simply smarter than they were yesterday. Intelligence is the ability to take information and put it to use. Smart is the ability to acquire information. So basically, it's the difference in using the information you have. **When you know better, you are supposed to do better!**

WHAT'S NEXT FOR ME SPECIFICALLY?

Politics aside, I have to live by my own standard. My success is defined by my own measurable objectives and everything I've built can cease to exist if I'm not continually finding ways to reinvent myself. I will always seek out ways to make my business more profitable for stability. I want to change the way our people think about life, about themselves, and about their self-worth. I am building the bridges and shortening the gap in assisting people in my community to see their future, by actualizing their dreams.

I am continuing to build my own personal brand. Although I am proud of my accomplishments; I'm far from finished. If I can accomplish what I've accomplished in the past 16 years, which is a relatively small amount of time in business, I am well on my way to achieve the greatness I desire.

Yes, I still need to sit down and re-evaluate my current businesses and map out how to take them to the next level. I am constantly asking myself **Why, Who, When, How, and Where do I want to go?** I can't very well tell you to follow **THE BLUEPRINT**, if I myself don't live by the same standard.

I need to ask myself do I want to continue to be in the business I'm in, take it a step further, or should I try a new business altogether.

My **BLUEPRINT** is my foundation. As I evaluate my mistakes I use them as an indicator to lead me to the next level of business. **"A man must be big enough to admit his mistakes, smart enough to profit from them, and strong enough to correct them."** ~John C. Maxwell

Whatever I decide to do next in business I will continue to look at the market to assure that I remain viable and relevant to what the next steps need to be.

People often ask me, "Are you comfortable where you are Tracey?" I smile always knowing the answer is that I can never be satisfied coming from where I come from. Anyone who knows me knows that I don't know how to define comfortable. I'm too busy chasing my dream. Yes, I'm successful by the standards of many, but by my standards I have a ways to go.

Do I still get fearful about certain elements of my life? Of course I do. When a new business endeavor falls upon my desk I get excited and scared at the same time. It's the rush of not knowing if I can pull the deal off; combined with the yes I can attitude that keeps my business fresh to me. My determination never lets me down and that continues to define me.

My last fearful deal was a $7 million dollar deal. I'd never worked on a $7 million dollar anything before, and I wasn't sure if I could pull it off. However, I found the courage and belief in myself, along with some positive encouragement from John, and we tackled the deal head on. We not only offered to buy the portfolio at $1.4 million, we raised the entire $1.4 million to complete the deal!

Although the initial deal fell through, a million dollar deal was born from the debris. The big deal set the stage for where I was unsure I could go. Yet it allowed me to lay the foundation and because of the learning process I'm encouraged to tackle deals of the same magnitude or larger.

What's next for me is getting people from my community and communities around the world to better understand business. I am going to redefine recidivism so that it's synonymous with **"From the Block to the Boardroom."** Believe it or not, I'm more committed to this cause than I am to the business politics in our community. My passion for this topic will allow me to travel around the United States sharing my methodology to change the way ex-offenders see themselves and rebuild their lives within society. I have pulled together a strong team behind this movement and we're beginning to lay the ground work to attain housing, job training and other beneficial means that are all important to the repositioning of an ex-offender into society. We're working in conjunction with some very reputable organizations who like us are excited about changing lives and mindsets.

One of those organizations is Wells Fargo. I'm working with them on the Trenton Public School Financial Literacy Program. The program is accredited by the state and falls in line with the guidelines of the "No Child Left Behind Act" program initiated under former President Bush. The program is mandated for 12th graders, but they've now established a program that will begin in the 4th grade and continue until the 12th grade laying out the foundation for financial freedom. It will be offered in both English and Spanish. The project planning is ongoing and we hope to implement it in the near future.

The hope is through programs like this one, we can start early enough to possibly deter individuals from ever becoming ex-offenders.

Having a criminal record doesn't have to be your death sentence and because I recognize this as fact, I'm providing a means that will allow individuals to stop signing their own death certificates. I'm not interested in just speaking about it, but working with organizations to implement change. We're in the process of pulling together some pretty amazing opportunities that will allow individuals to hope, dream, and take action. That's all an actualized plan is...it's the dream of someone who wanted it bad enough to make it a reality. That's the daily mission of From the Block to the Boardroom. We're supporting and creating programs for change for ex-offenders who wish to become honest law-abiding citizens. Individuals who deserve a chance because they recognize they're worth that chance. I'm willing to believe in anyone who puts forth the effort, works hard and chases their dreams. I will provide them **"THE BLUEPRINT."**

As for me personally, moving forward represents many new challenges. I am no longer the little boy who lost his way after his brother's death. I've evolved beyond the homeless teenager who hung out with models and wandered the streets of New York. I am light years away from the drugged out drug dealer and I'm eons more intelligent than the inmate who started to study African American history to get in touch with his heritage.

I remain a student of life and business at all times. I often play the role of teacher and confidant. I am a motivator, a mind changer, and on all occasions I am the man excited by the world of business and how cash flows.

I intend to inspire and empower people. I have used, mastered, and redefined **"THE BLUEPRINT."**

Now that I've shared it, all that's left is for you to take yourself ...**FROM THE BLOCK TO THE BOARDROOM.**

Get your suit or dress ready; we have a lot of networking to do. I'll meet you in the **BOARDROOM.**

At the completion of this book Tracey Syphax made history by being the first African American to receive the Entrepreneur of the Year Award from the Princeton Chamber of Commerce in its 51 years of existence.

CPSIA information can be obtained at www.ICGtesting.com
Printed in the USA
LVOW13s1722150714

394459LV00017B/1109/P

9 780985 029500